SPECIAL ACKNOWLEDGEMENT

SOCIAL VENTURE PARTNERS VANCOUVER

Nick Bedford

Christopher Morris

Ken Spencer

For their ongoing support of
Joe Calendino and the Yo Bro Yo Girl
Youth Initiative

JOE CALENDINO &

GARY LITTLE

TO

A FORMER HELLS ANGEL'S

STORY OF RECOVERY

AND REDEMPTION

HELL
AND BACK

L&C
press

Copyright © 2017 by Joe Calendino

L&C Press
Surrey, BC

Cataloguing data available from Library and Archives Canada
ISBN 978-0-9959407-0-3 (paperback)
ISBN 978-0-9959407-1-0 (ebook)
ISBN 978-0-9959407-2-7 (hardcover)

Produced by Page Two
www.pagetwostrategies.com
Cover and interior design by Peter Cocking
Cover and interior photos courtesy of Joe Calendino
Printed in Canada

18 19 20 21 22   6 5 4 3 2

To Dad. You continue to inspire me.

JOE CALENDINO

PREFACE

I FIRST met Joe Calendino when I worked as a counsellor and teacher of English at Templeton Secondary School in Vancouver's east side in the mid-1980s. Even then, Joe stood out, in a school population where it was not easy to stand out. There were high achievers, students who would go on to success in the worlds of academia and business. There were street-savvy kids, those you knew were going to succeed despite whatever life threw at them. There were the athletes and the artists. And in all of these groups, wherever you went at Templeton, you couldn't help but notice the Italian influence. Brash, warm and welcoming, these students were easily the most audible members of the school.

It was from this latter group and environment that Joe Calendino came. He certainly was not the highest achiever, either academically or athletically. He was not the most artistic, though I recall vividly the day Joe let me know that he would not be in class because he planned to land a role in *Rocky IV*, a Sylvester Stallone blockbuster being shot in Vancouver, not as an extra but as Stallone's body-double. Although Joe failed to land that role—he was a finalist—he worked on the film as an extra, receiving boxing shorts, a glove and a boot signed by the entire cast, Stallone included. Even at that stage of life, Joe thought big.

What separated Joe from the rest of the students was that special something only a few people have. In a school of high volume, Joe was not loud; in fact, he was quite soft-spoken. He was not physically intimidating, standing as he did at about five foot seven and weighing about 160 pounds. He was not driven to succeed, at least in the classroom. Joe had bounced around from school to school in Vancouver, a sign that he had run afoul of school authorities. But at Templeton he travelled a path that ensured he did not get into serious trouble with the principal or vice-principals.

That was the Joe Calendino I first got to know, the boy I exhorted to not go to Burnaby North Secondary School to fight every weekend, the young man who freely offered his opinions in the guidance class I team-taught. He was somebody others looked to when they needed a friend who had their back.

I lost touch with Joe when he graduated from Templeton. Twenty-eight years later, as I watched a Vancouver Police Department (VPD) presentation, I encountered him again. Aimed at deglamourizing gang life for students, the presentation was graphic, showing bullet holes riddling cars and bodies. Several of the gangsters were former students of mine. Among them, large as life, was Joe.

He was no longer the kid I remembered. His hair was longer, flecked with grey. He had filled out physically, and his face reflected something else, something I couldn't pinpoint at the time but came to understand later. He had lived life hard. Joe was now a full-patch Hells Angel, a Nomad, the VPD officers said. He was not just bad, but he was one of the baddest.

After I recovered from my shock and disappointment, I realized I was not entirely surprised Joe had ended up near the top of the criminal heap. He had always shown leadership qualities. I just wished he had found a different way to utilize them.

That was it. I never expected to see Joe again. We shared a city, but our worlds were as different as Jupiter is from Earth. Remarkably, though, our orbits were about to intersect.

I was working at the Vancouver School Board as an associate superintendent when two long-standing friends from Templeton Secondary, Jim Crescenzo, the school's drama teacher, and Walter Mustapich, one of the school's administrators, contacted me with a proposal they wanted to run by me, and said there was a former student they wanted to reintroduce. The student? Joe Calendino. We set a time so I could hear what they had to say.

Jim, Walter and Joe arrived punctually. Joe looked awful. He had a vicious-looking bandage on his right jaw that barely stemmed the leakage visible underneath. He wore a dark-grey suit over a white shirt open at the collar, and it was evident he had lost weight—a lot of weight. His hair was long and unkempt. But despite all this, there was something wonderfully familiar about him.

Joe and I hugged one another. I listened as Jim and Walter detailed what Joe was considering and explained why they wanted to support him. Joe wanted to work with kids. Help them avoid the life he had led. Make a difference. That kind of stuff. I'd heard it all before, hundreds of times, in different contexts. It's easy to get jaded. But this time was different. When Joe spoke, he was unsteady, definitely not the Joe I remembered. Nonetheless, there was something so compelling in what he said and how he said it that I knew this was an opportunity worth pursuing. In the pages that follow, you'll hear for yourself about Joe's life and his vision.

AUTHOR'S NOTE

Throughout the book, Joe Calendino's voice appears in *italics*. As well, I have chosen to represent myself in the third person, to maintain authorial distance and to reinforce the fact that this is Joe's story.

GARY LITTLE

1

NEWSCASTS said it was a bar frequented by gangs: Bar None, Vancouver, British Columbia. The bar was in hip Yaletown, once the city's industrial centre, now a panoply of glass-and-steel high-rises with embedded nightclubs and four-star restaurants.

Donny Roming was a mere two months short of his forty-first birthday. A full-patch member of the Nomads motorcycle club, the elite tranche within the notorious Hells Angels, he enjoyed a reputation as a straight shooter whose word was his bond. One of the brothers. In short, a guy you messed with at your peril. Donny was at Bar None on the night of March 9, 2001.

He hadn't gone there looking for trouble. He had gone, as he sometimes did, to see friends, have a few drinks and take care of some loose ends. Just before the bar's 2 a.m. closing time, Donny and a couple of other men inside the bar got into an argument. No one who witnessed the altercation could say later exactly what it was about or even who was involved. But you only had to know Donny to know that, whatever the situation, he was not going to back down from anybody.

The patrons who remained at that early hour saw Donny and the other men step outside. Soon afterward, the unmistakable *pop-pop-pop* retorts of gunfire punctuated the air. Screams shattered the night as people poured onto the street to see what had happened.

Donny lay badly injured on the cold asphalt. He struggled to fill his lungs with the moist air of that rainy March morning, frantic gasps that could be heard by the growing throng of onlookers. Paramedics took mere minutes to get there, but it already looked as if it might be too late. Donny's blood was draining onto the street, and with it his life. Another senseless killing in a city that had developed a reputation for senseless killings. Another casualty of gang life.

Across town, Joe Calendino, Donny's hang-around in the Nomads, was sleeping soundly. Joe was indebted to Donny for introducing him to the life he now led. Money. Women. Power. Drugs. Joe had it all—or so he thought. When the phone's ring cracked the silence that morning, everything was about to change.

The voice at the other end was panic-stricken. "Joe, you have to get here right away," the caller shouted. "It's Donny. He's been shot."

"What the fuck are you talking about, man? What the fuck! One more time, slowly."

"Donny's been shot. Right outside Bar None. Everyone who saw him says it doesn't look like he's going to make it. Joe, I wouldn't phone you at this time of the night, you know that, if it wasn't serious. You know I wouldn't."

"You better not be shitting me, or you'll be the next one." Joe slammed down the phone, sprang out of bed like the martial artist he was and threw on some clothes as he dashed for the door, almost forgetting the keys to his car and his ever-present Glock 9mm pistol in the process. His mind raced. This couldn't be right. Not Donny. Not his bro. The closest friend he had in the entire world.

Buildings raced by on either side, a blurry montage of gunmetal greys and mirror-like glass. The streets were slick with dew as Joe sped to Bar None. He drove for his life, and for Donny's. If he could just get there in time, he knew he could save his friend somehow.

Arriving at the nightclub, Joe was shocked to see the place behind a line of yellow police tape. Blood stained the ground nearby.

"Where is he? Where's Donny?" he yelled at the police.

"He's been taken to St. Paul's," a beefy constable responded. "But you better move fast. It's not looking good."

Jumping back into the driver's seat of his car, Joe laid a long patch of rubber as he made his exit. Only minutes later, he pulled up in front of the hospital. A solitary street-cleaning truck had deposited a swath of soap suds alongside the curb. Joe catapulted onto the sidewalk and up the modest flight of stairs that separated him from the hospital lobby. Not a soul in sight. The empty information kiosk served as a stark reminder that finding Donny at this time of morning was not going to be easy.

He raced down the hall toward Emergency. A nurse dressed in pale-blue scrubs sat at a dimly lit desk marked "Reception." Joe knew that, under the harsh fluorescent bulbs, he probably looked like some hyped-up character out of a *Goodfellas* sequel: sweating, hair askew, brown eyes crazed.

"I'm looking for Donny Roming. He was just brought in here. Where is he?"

"I'm sorry, sir. I'm not able to give out information on our patients."

"I don't give a shit what you can and cannot do. If you don't tell me where he is, I will go up and down every hallway in this hospital until I find him. I will destroy every fucking room if I have to. Where the fuck is he?"

The nurse burst into tears, and Joe was gone, sprinting madly to who knows where. A short time later he returned to Emergency, this time accompanied by a doctor.

"Take a seat, please," the doctor said quietly.

"I'm not taking any fucking seat," Joe yelled. "Where the fuck is Donny?"

Instinctively, the doctor stepped back. "I'm sorry, sir. Your friend is dead."

Joe let out a scream as he fell to his knees. His worst fears had been realized.

I first met Donny when I was a young man. I had built a reputation as a street fighter, a guy not to be messed with, although truth be told, I had had a couple of brutally tough fights in my life. One came early, with a guy named Alan Tolusso. I'll get back to that later. He and I squared off in front of friends, both his and mine. I remember it as if it were yesterday—the shouts, the excitement, the fact I wanted to kill him.

Joe's first encounter with Donny had been at a house party some twenty years earlier. Joe, barely turned seventeen years old, was strutting about the party with his friend Andy Amoroso as if he owned the place, a fact not lost on those in attendance. A giant of a man named Bodey found Joe's behaviour particularly irritating. Words were exchanged, and then, *smack*, Bodey nailed Joe with a right hand so powerful it knocked him about ten feet across the floor. Joe knew he had angered the wrong man, but there was no turning back. Not when it was this public. Not when Joe had a reputation to protect—or to earn, depending on your point of view.

But as the ringing in his head began to abate, allowing at least some semblance of clear thought, Joe saw Bodey reel from a right-hand punch he knew he had not delivered. That's when Joe noticed Donny Roming. The next thing Joe saw was Donny brandishing a beer bottle, which he smashed gruesomely on Bodey's skull. A heavy porcelain beer mug followed. Blood gushed everywhere, a mini-geyser of crimson spraying this way and that.

Joe could see that Donny was huge. Broad chest, long hair and several days of stubble on his chiselled face. The other thing that jumped out at him was Donny's smile. Even in the midst of the tension, Donny grinned as he ordered Bodey, "Leave the fucking kid alone." But there was nothing funny in Donny's presentation. His words were menacing. Joe knew if Bodey had thought for a millisecond that Donny was kidding, if he had dared to go at Joe a second time, his judgment would be proven wrong, perhaps dead wrong. No, there was nothing funny about it.

What followed amazed Joe even more. Donny grabbed an empty wine bottle from a nearby table and without commentary smashed it over his head—not Joe's head, not Bodey's head, but Donny's very own skull. With an understated wave of his hand, Donny then turned to Joe.

———

At that point I'm thinking I'm next. Instead, Donny looks at me and says matter-of-factly, "See you later, kid." That was my cue to leave. I got up and walked out. I can see the events of that night in my mind as if they occurred yesterday.

———

Based on the events of that evening, one more name was added to the already extensive Donny Roming fan club. That name? Joe Calendino.

———

Donny Roming was the one individual who truly taught me the art of war, what it is to be a member of the big gang. He lived for the club, and as it turned out, tragically, he died for the club.

I spent the better part of an entire year with Donny. He respected me and loved me as only one brother can truly love another brother. He had an enormous sense of humour and made me laugh repeatedly, often to the point where I lost sight of the many stresses of my own life, including my quest to be a full-patch member. He was just great to be around.

Donny also taught me something about women, not that he necessarily intended to or had to. I was doing just fine on my own, thank you very much. But when I saw him with one woman after another, I realized this was something else in the gang life that had great appeal for me as well. I wanted what he had. Being Italian, I suppose this passion for the opposite sex resides deep in the genes. At least, that is what I tell myself. Make no mistake about it, though; Donny led the way, even though he had about as much Italian in his genetic structure as I have Inuit in mine. He was a true stallion. He not only showed me how important it was to be as tough as nails when the occasion called for it, he also showed me what it was to have that special something that appeals to members of the opposite sex if a man is truly respected. And boy, did he ever have that special something.

I suppose our coming together was fate. After all, I met Donny while I was still a wet-behind-the-ears teen, the night he saved me from a serious beating at the hands of that monster of a man. Twenty years later, there I was, an aspiring full-patch one percenter who was turning his back on a successful business career and the values that had been inculcated in me as a young boy. This was not Donny's doing. It was my doing. Donny was merely the catalyst, the mentor, who would help me get where I wanted to go.

All of this made the phone call that night that much harder to bear. I know I will never forget it or get over it. I can still hear the ringing of the phone shattering the dark silence every time I allow my mind to wander back.

I still find myself wondering, "Would things have turned out differently for Donny had I been there?" I will never know.

2

PRINCE Rupert, British Columbia, is so far from the town of Mangone, on the west coast of southern Italy, that if you were to ask a citizen of that Italian region where "Rupert" is located on a map, they could just as easily point to the British Isles or Germany as to Canada. Few would correctly guess that Prince Rupert is a city located at the northwestern terminus of the Canadian National Railway on British Columbia's massive west coast—unless they have relatives in that part of the world.

Wet to the point that it boasts the name "Rainmakers" for several of its sports teams, Prince Rupert is considered one of Canada's soggiest cities, with over a hundred inches of annual rainfall. A South African family made headlines when they sought permanent resident status in Rupert because three of four family members suffered from porphyria, a rare skin disorder that causes the human body to develop a serious allergy to sun. They could not have chosen a better location to safeguard their condition. Yet proud residents will tell you that when the sun finally does break through, Rupert is one of the most breathtaking places on our planet.

Like many BC cities, Prince Rupert is a resource-based community. Recently, it has been the focus of much speculation regarding the transport of Alberta bitumen through its nexus of railways and deep-sea port. The Pacific Northwest LNG project, approved by the federal government in September 2016, would see liquid natural gas moving through Prince Rupert on its journey to the rich markets of Asia. If the project comes to fruition, the city will receive a jolt of economic activity paired with ongoing debate and virtually guaranteed protests about potential environmental devastation.

Salmon and halibut remain the area's fishing staples, but Rupert is equally well known for its vast forests and vibrant logging industry. In the summertime, sleek white cruise ships ply the waters of the Inside Passage before docking in the city itself. Disembarking passengers are wowed by the natural beauty of the area and grateful for the opportunity to take a stroll.

Immortalized in literature and song, Canada's railways have played a major role in building the country and in binding one region to the next. Rupert is no exception. While Vancouver received much publicity in March 1887 when the first passenger train rolled into the city on the newly constructed Canadian Pacific Railway, the Grand Trunk Pacific Railway was equally important to the burgeoning commerce and communities that lined it in the north.

Most importantly—for our purposes, at least—Prince Rupert is where Frank Calendino found himself on a typically overcast day in July 1964. Frank had arrived in Canada—in Vancouver, to be precise—several years earlier. His pockets were empty that day in July, his heart full of hope.

Frank had settled in Vancouver with his parents, his brothers Ralph and Pietro, and his sisters Liliana, Autha and Elda. He enrolled in Britannia Secondary in 1957, lasting exactly one year there. Frank was more interested in making friends than in making verbs agree with nouns. Nevertheless, he developed a sufficient mastery of English to become the centre of several social groups, made up of kids like himself who were drawn to the music of that period—Elvis being the king of them all—and to the opportunities that the buoyant economy presented.

Although Frank might have exhibited the grace of a gazelle on the dance floor, off it he had the heart of a lion. When he and his brother Ralph found work on the rails, they meandered north to Prince George, a central Interior hub city with a budding pulp-and-paper industry and lots of logging nearby. The brothers were neither afraid of hard work nor intimidated by the men who performed it.

Then in his early twenties, Frank cut an impressive figure. He had the features common to the Mediterranean region from which he had emigrated. His hair, curly, jet-black and somewhat long for the 1950s, swept down the nape of his neck. His dark brown eyes radiated warmth when he smiled, intensity and smouldering anger when his mood shifted. Frank was tough, and he made sure that everyone he came into contact with knew it. "Don't challenge me," his demeanour said. And few people did. "Don't ever let anyone see weakness," he would later counsel his three children. "Never! They'll just take advantage of you."

The brothers Calendino soon got bored with the isolation of working on the rails, Ralph ditching the job a month or two before Frank decided to do the same. They made their way to Kitimat, a resource-based town on British Columbia's coast that was home to the giant Alcan aluminum smelter.

Frank's life took an unexpected turn when he developed Bell's palsy and had to return to Vancouver for treatment. Two months of medical appointments and incessant interventions later, he headed back to join Ralph in Kitimat. Work at the smelter, much like his experience on the rails, was not for Frank. He disliked the smoke and the dust spewed by this industrial giant and decided to seek employment elsewhere. Before long, he landed work with a maintenance firm that was making a name for itself in town. One of the principal shareholders was his older brother, Ralph.

When Ralph took over the running of the maintenance company and moved back to Prince Rupert, Frank joined him there. Their working relationship did not last long—not that there was any enmity involved. Frank found it difficult working for someone else, plain and simple. Realizing that he had to carve out his own niche, be his own man, he launched the White Bear Maintenance Company, a not-so-subtle signal that Ralph had better take the competitive instincts of his younger brother seriously.

Despite White Bear's schedule requiring Frank to work steady nights, he found time to patrol Prince Rupert's party circuit. Women were drawn to his easy charm and smashing good looks. Young and old, they vied for Frank's attention. One such woman, nine years his junior, went by the name of Nerina Carnivale. Frank "swept her off her feet," as his younger brother, Pietro, would recall later in describing this period of Frank's life.

Several days after meeting Nerina at a party, Frank strolled into the Third Avenue market, where he knew she worked. Securing the essentials for his evening meal (Frank still valued the wonderful Italian tradition of buying fresh bread, meat and produce whenever possible), he approached the checkout counter where Nerina stood poised to process his order.

With deliberate flair, Frank placed his items on the checkout conveyor belt. As Nerina rang them up, it wasn't clear whether he was studying her or the rising bill. When she presented him with the final tally, though, he saw she had made an error. He worked too hard night after night to line the pockets of a store owner. He had been overcharged—no ifs, ands or buts about it.

"Sorry," he said in Italian. "This is wrong." A smile spread across his face. He pointed to an item on the bill. Nerina countered his claim.

"You are wrong. This is correct," she replied in Italian also. "I should know; I work here."

Nerina, having arrived in Canada only a few months earlier, was more at ease speaking Italian than English. She too smiled warmly by way of response. Whether she was right or not, she really didn't care. She was enjoying this volley and return with a handsome man several years her senior. This newcomer to town could have passed as a movie star, she thought. In her young eyes, he had that kind of celebrity charm.

"Well," Frank said, "I'll tell you what. You give me your phone number and we'll call it even. How about that?"

"I suppose I can do that," Nerina replied, trying to appear nonchalant. "But if I do, we'll only be pretending to be even, because you know and I know that you are wrong." She laughed. Frank Calendino's face lit up as well, his smile stretching from one side clear across to the other. Nerina was only sixteen when they met in November 1964, Frank a well-travelled twenty-five. But there was something between them that overcame the age difference. Soon they were in love.

Frank was a born risk taker. As a young boy in Mangone, he was fearless. Even as the bombs of World War II racked the countryside around his hometown, Frank refused to heed air-raid sirens imploring people to seek shelter. He was also known to have climbed the outside stone wall of the church on more than one occasion in order to ring the bell, usually a signal to the townspeople that one of their compadres had died or been killed in action. Only mischievous Frank knew the truth: the town's population had not decreased by even a factor of one that day. Frank had been known as well to put moist green wood into the teacher's wood-burning stove, making the air so bad that class had to be suspended for an hour or more while the smoke cleared. Clearly, a career as a scholar was not in Frank's future.

Nerina was smitten, and she was ready to make a bigger gamble of her own: she agreed to marry Frank. They were wed a year later, two days after Christmas, despite the objections raised by Nerina's parents. It was not so much that they disliked Frank; they simply felt their daughter was too young to get married, especially to a groom nearly a decade her senior. In the end, though, love prevailed.

IT DIDN'T TAKE long for the young couple to begin their family. Son Joe was born in 1966, middle child Ralph in 1967 and daughter Eva in 1971. Like other young parents, Frank and Nerina would do anything for their children; they loved them more than life itself.

From the earliest days, there was something that connected Joe to his father. Joe had the kind of relentless energy that keeps parents perpetually alert and perpetually tired. "Someday, Frank," Nerina would say, "Joey will slow down. Someday." Truth be told, she wondered if that day would ever come. It had certainly not come for her husband, and he was fast approaching thirty years of age.

Life in Prince Rupert was challenging for the Calendinos. Nerina had been able to adapt to the rain and the various shades of grey that accompanied it, but Frank never got used to the incessant cloud cover. Winter temperatures rarely dipped below the freezing point, but to a man from the Mediterranean, even those levels cut to the core. Frank felt the cold while other residents of the community were commenting on how unseasonably warm things were in mid-December or January, and the "blazing" heat of July affected him only mildly.

Frank found time to socialize, gathering friends around him like some people collect pieces of china or souvenirs from foreign lands. But he also had concerns about the demands his new business placed on him. Sure, he was able to make a living with his new venture, but it was exacting a toll on his young family. He was almost always out of the house, when he would rather have been home playing with his children.

When several of Nerina's siblings moved south to Kamloops, Frank and Nerina decided to pack up their family and do the same. For starters, the weather there was hotter and drier. Kamloops more closely resembled arid Arizona than it did the verdant forests of the west coast. It was also a town of opportunity. Despite the people of British Columbia having recently elected their first NDP government, under the leadership of Dave Barrett, Kamloops remained a bastion of free enterprise. Frank expected to duplicate, if not exceed, his previous success with White Bear.

Unfortunately, that was not to be. Frank soon discovered that he was not alone in trying to secure maintenance contracts in the community. Long-established businesses had pretty much cornered the market. In addition, those businesses had built relationships over time with their many clients, something not easy for a newcomer to do in any of the small Interior towns that dotted the landscape.

Still, the Calendinos were happy. Nerina was surrounded by her family, which meant the world to her. Young Joe struck up a friendship with his cousin Tony, and together they expended energy the way Frank had as a young boy growing up in Mangone. Joe and Tony explored the nearby sandy hills, imagining themselves intrepid explorers or fearless cowboys of the first order.

"Joe was like a brother to me, the brother I never had," Tony recalls today. "We were inseparable."

It was in Kamloops that Joe began his formal public schooling. The family tells a story that speaks not only to his character but equally to that of his mother. Although he exhibited the rambunctiousness that had been the hallmark of his father at the same age, Joe was sensitive. It was not entirely surprising, therefore, when he came home from Grade 1 one day with tears streaming from his eyes. He reported to his mother, "Mamma, the teacher keeps pulling my ears. She picks on me in front of the other kids. I can't stand her. I don't want to go back to her class. It's not fair what she does to me."

Even at that age, Joe had a developed sense of right and wrong. Having his ears pulled by a heartless teacher was wrong. His mother agreed. Furious, she made an appointment to see the teacher.

"How would you like it," Nerina challenged the teacher, on the other side of the desk, "if I did the same to you?" Compelled by forces that to this day she cannot fully fathom, Nerina reached across the desk and, to demonstrate her point, grabbed a handful of the teacher's hair. To her shock, she came away holding a wig. The teacher was angry and embarrassed. Nerina, for her part, coolly laid the wig on the teacher's desk, picked herself up from the chair and made her way out of the school. Joe's ears were off limits from that day forward.

Around the same time that Nerina was protecting the interests of their eldest son, Frank ran afoul of the authorities in the Kamloops region and was sentenced to time in jail. Not just any jail, mind you. Frank was shuttled off to British Columbia's most infamous prison, commonly known as the BC Pen, for his misdeeds.

Joe, like his younger brother and sister, was too young to fully comprehend what was happening to the family. What he did know was that his dad was gone, and his mother wore her grief like a first-time poker player trying to bluff a bad hand. The spark that Nerina usually displayed was nowhere in evidence.

A few months later, Nerina loaded up the family car for the long and arduous drive to Vancouver. Their route included the highway that ran through British Columbia's notorious Fraser Canyon, a geographic oddity resulting from years of the pounding, erosive effects of the Fraser River. The stated purpose of the trip was to visit Frank in prison in New Westminster, but the family was really heading to Vancouver to see other relatives—of whom there were many—and to consider a full-time move to the city, something Frank and Nerina had talked about before his arrest. The kids were excited about the car trip that lay ahead, but the trip was never completed. As Nerina headed south, the car loaded with her three children and her niece Maria, a semi-trailer truck travelling too fast on a dangerous stretch of road crossed the yellow line dividing the northbound and southbound lanes. Nerina swerved violently to avoid a collision, then struggled to regain control of her vehicle. Her efforts were futile. The late-model station wagon skidded off the highway and pitched headlong down an embankment. The children were tossed about inside the car like popcorn exploding to life inside a microwave—all except for one. Little Eva, still clutching her security blanket, was thrown from the vehicle and landed on the shoulder of the highway. She barely had a scratch.

The sickening crumple of metal continued as the car plunged down the embankment. Finally, an eerie silence descended upon the scene. As Eva let loose a penetrating scream, a man dressed in white from head to toe appeared out of nowhere on a white horse.

Years later, Eva recounts this story as if it were yesterday.

"What's wrong, little girl? Are you all by yourself?" the man asked.

Reeling from the shock of what had happened, Eva continued screaming by way of response. "My mommy, my mommy" was all she could muster. She pointed to a break in the trees. The sheared stumps that dotted the landscape led directly to the wreck.

Once he had ensured that Eva was okay and instructed her not to move from the safety of the highway's shoulder, the man made his way down the embankment. What must have been a terrible sight met his eye. The three children inside lay in a tangled heap, and Nerina was slouched behind the steering wheel, in shock and unable to move. Ribbons of blood flowed across the upholstery.

Knowing there was little he could do at the scene, the mystery "white knight" (as he became known to the family) rode off for help. It was as quick in arriving as could be expected in this remote area, though the wait felt like an eternity to those whose lives hung in the balance. That was the last the family would ever hear of the man on the horse. To this day they do not know his identity, but they are quick to attribute their survival to him. "When I think back to the accident," Eva says, "I don't know where that guy came from. We were in the middle of the fricking highway in the middle of nowhere." She shakes her head in amazement.

The paramedics remarked later that it was a miracle no one had been killed—though everyone other than Eva suffered significant injuries. The area around Joe's eye had been sliced open and his arm broken; Ralph suffered a broken leg; Nerina had a broken arm and a broken leg; and cousin Maria had her head cut open.

From this trauma and the trauma of Frank's incarceration, the family recovered slowly. As soon as their injuries had healed, close to a year after the horrific accident, Nerina moved her three children to Vancouver. By this time, Frank had been released from prison, and the family settled in working-class East Vancouver. Home to many immigrants like themselves, East Van was definitely hardscrabble at the time. Kids grew up quickly, sometimes too quickly. Parents were frequently so involved in trying to scratch out a living that they had little energy left for the challenges of child rearing. Especially in "traditional" families—Dad at work, Mom at home looking after the children—language barriers frequently meant that the mother felt isolated, cut off from the traditional supports that make parenting a joy rather than a series of painful obstacles and setbacks.

Despite these challenges—or perhaps because of them—the kids who came out of East Vancouver shared a number of positive traits. They were loved by parents who were as quick to utilize the rod as they were oblivious to the latest in child-rearing techniques. East side kids were raised to understand boundaries, even if they didn't always adhere to them. They frequently valued education, a fact reinforced by parents whose own educations had more often than not been truncated. They prized their immediate communities, finding their cultures familiar and reassuring. It was not uncommon for youngsters in East Vancouver to have travelled with their families to the "old country" (Italy or China or the former Yugoslavia) without ever having visited Kitsilano or crossed the Lions Gate Bridge to the suburbs of the North Shore.

Over the years, East Vancouver spawned many notables: professional athletes, leaders in the business community, a judge in British Columbia's Supreme Court, and even a premier of the province, the Right Honourable Dave Barrett. The neighbourhood also gave rise to a member of British Columbia's legislature by the name of Pietro Calendino: Frank's younger brother and Joe's uncle.

The Calendinos fit into the community perfectly. They purchased an unpretentious house in the vicinity of Commercial and East 22nd, a three-floor home that at the time was comparable in price to the going rates in Kamloops or Prince Rupert. Today, in the city's crazy real estate market, the austere Calendino home would easily sell for over $1 million.

Nerina found work as a cook, first at Mocha restaurant—now Federico's—and then at Tommy O's, a fixture on Commercial Drive. Here the players and management of the city's professional hockey team, the Vancouver Canucks, could often be found dining on the finest pasta anywhere in the city, thanks in no small measure to Nerina's culinary skills. As a second job, Nerina worked at Nelson's Linen and Laundry on 4th Avenue. Whatever obstacles lay in her path, Nerina Calendino was convinced she could overcome them through hard work and force of will. Why not? The formula had always worked for her in the past.

Frank found employment in the steel-fabricating industry. While he loved his children and his wife, he was as far from the stereotype of the nurturing dad as Ozzie Nelson is from Ozzy Osbourne. Frank left most of the child-rearing responsibilities to Nerina. Between the coffee bars of Commercial Drive—the Italian part of the city in those days, where cards and money exchanged hands freely—and the horses at Exhibition Park (today the Hastings Race Track), he found many reasons to be away from home. Frank's kids knew their dad loved them and had their best interests at heart, even if he was absent for considerable chunks of their lives. They accepted, even embraced, his simple but heartfelt philosophy: Always look after everyone in your family, because when all is said and done, family is all you've got.

After a while, Frank and Nerina launched their own business, a maintenance company similar in design and intent to White Bear Maintenance Company of Prince Rupert. Their enterprise enjoyed considerable success, but it demanded a commitment from every member of the family. After a full day of school, the kids would arrive home to chores that awaited them. From a very young age, Eva was charged with cooking dinner. In addition, she, Ralph and Joe were expected to complete any schoolwork they had before heading out with Mamma and Papa to assist with the dusting, vacuuming and sorting through of garbage that would leave the offices they tended to sparkling the next morning when their clients arrived at work. Frank and Nerina would finally fold the business in 1991. Joe and his siblings were adults by then and had not worked with their parents for some time, but the lessons they learned on the job would remain with them.

THE NEIGHBOURHOOD WHERE the Calendinos lived was more Manchester than Mayberry. Despite the rows of tomato plants and zucchinis grown in backyard gardens, there existed an unmistakable grittiness. Kids were allowed significant freedom compared with today's children, but that carried with it a price. Their classroom was the street every bit as much as it was the schoolroom. The street was where Joe excelled. As he grew older, his neighbourhood expanded in size and complexity.

First off, Joe made sure that no one pushed him around. Still smarting from the ear pulling by the Kamloops teacher, he vowed never to be humiliated by anyone again. His air of machismo resulted in other boys being drawn to Joe like kids learning the game of soccer are drawn to the ball—a sport, by the way, that Joe played exceedingly well. On the pitch, as elsewhere, he was fuelled by an intensity that mirrored the fires within. People who observed him at the time note today that if Joe had stayed with the game, he could have had a future in it, perhaps even at the professional level. But that was not to be; there were too many other distractions.

Learning to play the drums was no different. Even though he had never heard of Ginger Baker and had only had a passing knowledge of The Who's Keith Moon, Joe's "attack style" on the skins was reminiscent of those Hall of Fame rockers. He could carry a beat, sure, but he would leave the subtleties of drumming to the jazz musicians. He wanted the drums to scream, to cry uncle. Years later, he would fight his adversaries with the same unfettered frenzy.

As for school, Joe took over where his father had left off. He was capable. That much is clear from the comments of teachers such as Mrs. Una Fester, Joe's Grade 7 teacher at Lord Selkirk Elementary School. She remembers with great lucidity the Joe Calendino she knew as part of a rambunctious class of over thirty students.

"Joe had all kinds of ability," she says today. "He was a good boy, energetic and compassionate. But even then he was not overly focused on his studies. He seemed more interested in sports and music and being part of the gang. He exhibited real leadership qualities, though." After a pause, she continues. "Oh, yes. He was developing a serious interest in girls—and they in him. It didn't matter where Joe went, there were always several girls who followed him around—or so it seemed."

Una Fester learned of Joe's notoriety in later years. "I was as surprised as anyone when I first heard what had happened to Joe, the Hells Angels and all that," she says. "I bumped into him one day on the street. He looked very much the part of the successful businessman, in a beautiful blue suit. I had no idea how he'd made his money. But I am not surprised he has now turned his life around and is making a difference for young people. That caring dimension was the other side of Joe's character."

There was no doubt the transition from Kamloops to Vancouver had been rough. The Calendinos had left behind the simplicity of small-town life for the harshness of Vancouver's east side. They had left behind many family members too, and Joe missed them all terribly.

––––––––––

Vancouver at the time: I don't want to call it moving into the fire, but it was certainly moving into an old-school environment, the school of hard knocks. Mac-jacket- and Dayton-wearing, bearded guys in Grade 7, for Christ's sake. I don't know what happened to the children from that area, but they came in very large sizes. Many of them are dead and gone now. I was at Lord Selkirk school, right in the thick of it—East 22nd and Commercial.

The impact of the early upheavals in Joe's life—the family's moves around the province, the horrific traffic accident, his dad's incarceration—was considerable. But Joe loved his father, even idolized him, and in a very real sense he wanted to be exactly like his papa. Joe tells a story that speaks to the bond they shared.

One day, still new to Lord Selkirk and to the city, Joe reported to his father that there was a boy who was tormenting him. "He punches me, kicks me, calls me names—you name it, he does it, Dad." As he recounted these events to his father, young Joe's eyes rimmed with tears. His father focused a hardening gaze on Joe.

"Don't ever let that happen, son. Ever. You must never let anyone—anyone—have that kind of power or control over you."

With that, Frank ushered Joe into the family car. They were headed back to the school. That much was clear to young Joe. Business was business, and to Frank it was obvious that this score needed settling.

Joe was terrified that his dad was going to inflict serious damage on the school bully, maybe even beat the bully so badly that Frank would end up back in prison. If that was the case, Joe wanted no part of it. They drove slowly along the edge of the school grounds. A small group of students stood there, their eyes fixed on the Calendinos.

Joe stammered, "That's him there, Papa, the one with the red hat."

"That's the kid who's picking on you, son?" his dad replied. Conflicted, Joe hesitated. "Joe, I'm talking to you. You're sure that's the kid? Don't lie to me. I want the truth."

Joe nodded slowly, his heart racing.

Frank slammed his foot on the accelerator. The car cata-pulted forward, and Frank skidded it into position, blocking the road: East Vancouver's version of *Starsky and Hutch*. Other parents were picking up their children, but not a single one laid a finger on the horn to get Frank to move—undoubtedly wise under the circumstances.

Frank turned to his son. "Joe, you are going to walk over to that kid right now and let him know with your fists—no words—that he is never to pick on you again. Got that? Never again. Now, get going."

With that, he opened the passenger door and pushed Joe out.

Joe did not say anything. He made a beeline for the bully and threw his best left-right combination square in the boy's face. Down he went. The bully rolled himself up off the gravel surface and crawled away, looking fearfully over his shoulder to ensure that neither Joe nor Joe's dad was in pursuit.

Joe headed back to the car.

"You see, Joe," Frank stated, a hint of a smile on his face, "bullies are tough when you don't stand up to them. Challenge 'em, though, and they fold. They fold like a mouldy tent. Come apart at the seams. Let that be a lesson that you hold on to for the rest of your life."

Frank was right. The school bully never picked on Joe again.

3

GLADSTONE Secondary School is located on a tiny stretch of road midway between Nanaimo Street and Victoria Drive in Vancouver. Directly to the south is Kingsway Avenue, a sprawling thoroughfare of tiny stores that span the spectrum of commercial offerings: tire shops, massage parlours, beauty salons and restaurants of every description. While modern malls, including the cavernous Metrotown, abut Kingsway today, it has never fully lost the character that defined it as one of the major arterial routes into the city in the 1940s and 1950s. Kingsway has always been more *West Side Story* than west side tony. It remains home to many families making their way into Canadian society alongside others who are doing their level best to make their way out of the neighbourhood.

Gladstone itself hearkens back to the late 1950s, when schools were built from cinder block, utilitarian and impressively uninviting. "Arctic cold" might be the best description of the architecture. Nonetheless, Gladstone has launched many local successes. A fabulously successful businessman named Nelson Skalbania graduated from the school, as did Wayson

Choy, a celebrated Canadian writer, and Ken Lum, a gifted visual artist who has won international recognition for his work. Lum has also earned a certain degree of notoriety for a recent project, his *Monument for East Vancouver*—a towering cross with the words "East" and "Van" intersecting at the junction of the cross itself.

For Joe Calendino, as for most kids growing up on the east side of Vancouver, the East Van cross was a symbol of pride. Drawn proudly on covers of school notebooks and spray painted on fences and walls, it appeared long before Lum's monument made its appearance. "East Van" meant that you were working class. It meant that if somebody took you lightly— especially if that person was from the affluent west side of the city or, worse yet, from arch-rival Burnaby—there would be a price to pay. The symbol meant respect.

As an incoming Grade 8 student at Gladstone Secondary, Joe did not stand out. He was no longer the cock of the walk, a role he had assumed with pride during his Grade 6 and 7 years. The image he'd carved out after his initial encounters with bullies, of being the baddest and toughest kid in a school full of bad and tough kids, might have worked at Lord Selkirk, but it did not work at Gladstone. For him, even to try would have been like an untested amateur bantamweight boxer hoping to strike fear into the ranks of top-level professional heavyweights.

Nevertheless, Joe was undeterred. He found trouble the way most students find their way to their new locker assignment: the route is a little challenging at first, and then it becomes second nature. Joe did not look up to the acknowledged leaders at Gladstone, the president of the students' council or the captain of the school's basketball team. Rather, he looked up to the young men who routinely skipped class to cluster just inches from school property, smoking cigarettes and other inhalable products, and driving cars that had been modified to deliver more power than mere stock engines could. The guys Joe looked up to personified "bad," even if some of them were decent human beings beneath their badass personas. It was also at Gladstone that Joe met Andy Amoroso, who would become his lifelong best friend.

Going from Selkirk to Gladstone was a shock wave. We had our clique. And the guys I ended up with were the very same guys I mentioned earlier—the Mac-wearing, Dayton-wearing, Harley-belt-buckle-wearing type of guy. This type of guy was very prevalent in those days. Role models wearing golf shirts tucked neatly into their pressed pants either did not exist or, if they did, I didn't notice them. They were not the type of people I wanted to connect with.

The goal Joe set for himself was clear: to be the toughest student in all of Gladstone by the time he hit Grade 12—if not earlier. In the meantime, he continued fine-tuning his interests. His love of drumming remained as steady as a 4/4 beat on an electronic drum machine. He excelled on the soccer pitch for community teams Killarney and Grandview. He even tried his hand at hockey, though when he realized there was little future for him in that sport, he quickly abandoned it in favour of boxing at the Shamrock Boxing Club. He also, at Kel Lee's Academy of Martial Arts, pursued martial arts—an activity he knew would serve him well in achieving his singular school goal.

As had his father, Joe loved the social side of school. Also like Frank, he eschewed scholarship.

Some guys love phys. ed. or mathematics or English; my favourite course was Fighting 101.

Things reached the point where Joe spent more time with the administrators at the school than he did with his classroom teachers. Finally, the school's vice-principal, Dr. Ted Hunt, a celebrated BC Sports Hall of Fame athlete and a no-nonsense old-school educator, called Joe into his office.

"Joe," Hunt began, "I've noticed something lately. You seem happy. You have lots of friends. You are even seen in the hall-ways of the school on occasion, sometimes in your classes. Sadly, Gladstone just isn't working for you, or you for it. We've given you every opportunity to succeed, but it's time we try something else. You get the idea?"

Joe nodded. He not only got the idea, he had a strong sense of what was coming next.

"I'll be transferring you to another school, where you'll get a chance to start fresh with a clean slate. Maybe this time you'll realize the potential people have told us you have but we've seen little evidence of. That means you'll have to attend class—at least as a starting point—every day. In class, on time, all the time."

For most students, this would have been a terrible blow. Joe took it in stride. In fact, he found little in what Gladstone's VP said to disagree with, and today he describes Dr. Hunt as one of a handful of educators he truly looked up to in Vancouver's public school system. Chances are Joe saw a bit of himself in Ted Hunt. Both of them are straight shooters.

Things didn't get a whole lot better at Joe's next stop or at the succession of stops that followed. Killarney, Sir Charles Tupper, John Oliver, Streetfront Alternative, Killarney... the names rolled like encyclopedia entries one into another. The merry-go-round of schools Joe attended began spinning faster and faster.

And, of course, I got kicked out of every single one.

Joe did not lack intelligence. Nor did he lack discipline. He was committed to those endeavours that were of interest to him: Martial arts. Boxing. Being the toughest kid in all of East

Vancouver. What he lacked was a single goal that included the academic side of school.

Throughout these years, Joe's father remained a massive influence in his life. As Joe saw it, Frank Calendino exhibited an assemblage of qualities to which he aspired. Honesty. Courage. Work ethic. Toughness. These were the qualities that would serve Joe so well, on the one hand, and very nearly destroy his life, on the other.

Like many men of his generation, Frank was not afraid to get his hands dirty. He worked long hours, often at jobs he disliked. That was the role of a father in those days, one Frank never questioned. Part of his understanding of what it meant to be tough was doing whatever it took to support your family. But he liked to enjoy himself too. "Work hard, play hard" seemed to be Frank Calendino's motto.

As a teenager, Joe had already absorbed two of Frank's constituent tenets to live by. Joe feared no one. He never walked from a fight. In fact, he was usually the one to initiate it. He also partied hard. What started as a weekend routine—party, fight, chase girls, then party and fight some more—eventually became his mid-week routine as well. It was during this time that Joe had his legendary fight with a guy named Alan Tolusso. He still marvels at the memory.

The way it started was almost like something you would see in a movie. I was with all my buddies, and there were fights going on all over the place. You could say it was something of a blood-fest.

I was training in boxing at the time and was afraid of no one. I didn't think much of it when I bumped into Alan, a six-foot-two firefighter who lived in the neighbourhood. Well, truth be told, I bumped the wrong guy. He was twenty-three at the time and was not going to be embarrassed by some snot-nosed kid. He scowled at me and then muttered something to the effect of "So you think you're tough, you little shit!"

My friend Isaac jumped into the middle of this confrontation. "Okay," Isaac says, "let's do the crowd, Rock [his nickname for Joe]." Pretty soon, a crowd starts to form. Isaac continues his chatter, a kind of amped-up Don King trying to orchestrate the next heavyweight championship bout of the world. Trouble was I was the one who was going have to fight it while Isaac remained a safe distance away, still chattering.

Alan and I went at it. Boy, did we go at it. Toe to toe for ten solid minutes, and that is no exaggeration. We threw everything we had at each other: kicks to the head, punches thrown from every conceivable angle, even wrestling holds. From one car to the next we continued to scrap, throwing each other into various vehicles as we went.

Eventually, two guys broke us up, kind of like two linesmen in hockey who step in when it's clear the two combatants have nothing left in their tanks. Alan and I were out to win at first, not kill each other, just win. Then I snapped. I grabbed a beer bottle, smashed its neck so that it became a formidable weapon, and began to make my way toward Alan to stab him. I mean, I had totally lost it!

Suddenly, and without noticing the beer bottle in my hand, Alan stopped me dead in my tracks and said, "Hey, that was the greatest fight of my life." He extended a hand to me. I was stunned, totally confused. He had just said something that meant more to me than anything else in my life to that point. He had affirmed my existence as a fighter.

I disposed of the jagged bottle, accepted his hand and shook it. We continued to look at each other, menace and bravado replaced by respect. People were applauding, clapping and whistling. There was not just one winner; there were two.

If I could live that fight again, I would be in heaven. Over twenty years later, people still come up to me and talk about *the time Alan Tolusso and I engaged in the best fight they had ever seen. Over twenty years later. It's like the Rumble in the Jungle or the Thrilla in Manila—at least in the annals of East Vancouver street fights.*

Joe eventually found his way to Templeton Secondary School on Vancouver's east side. Most people would have decided that school was not in the cards for them by then. Not Joe. If nothing else, he was a survivor. He approached his new school with the same insouciance he had displayed in the six high schools that preceded it. He walked with a swagger. He wore a leather jacket and menacing Dayton boots that communicated to others in a kind of Dirty Harry way, "Go ahead, make my day." He demanded and commanded respect.

Templeton was like most of the other schools Joe had inhabited. It was, and is today, a comprehensive school, which means it offers not only academic programs leading to university entry but also a vast array of other courses: shop-based options such as automotives, electronics, woodwork and metalwork; arts courses focused on either visual or performing arts; business subjects such as marketing, management and communications; and music courses. It must be said that even if Joe had not allowed his drumming to lapse, he would not have been caught dead playing in the school band.

The courses he took didn't matter a whole lot to Joe, anyway. He just wanted to complete his high school diploma in the shortest time possible. He wanted to get school over with so he could get on with his life. But at Templeton, something happened that most people would say was nothing short of a miracle. Joe Calendino did not get kicked out. Some at the school would have been happy to see him go, but a couple of staff members took him under their wings, most notably Jim Crescenzo, himself a graduate of Templeton and the school's revered drama teacher.

Crescenzo instantly commanded Joe's respect. Like Joe, he was of Italian heritage. Jim had grown up in the same general neighbourhood and had himself faced adversity at a young age, having lost his father. Furthermore, Jim in his day had been an accomplished soccer player and a social magnet at Templeton, popular with all students but especially with girls, who found his love of life and Italian good looks difficult to resist. The big difference was that Jim had been a dedicated student where Joe was anything but.

Jim saw something of himself in Joe as well. Had Jim not received the benefit of early supportive influences, such as the genial and respected principal Lou Rosse and teachers Geoff Jopson and Bob McKay, he might have followed the same problematic pathway as his new charge. Mr. C., as the students called him, was not going to let this Calendino kid get away on him.

Joe began attending classes—not full-time, but with enough frequency that he was allowed to remain in school. While his marks were not in danger of drawing the attention of Ivy League recruiters, they were a step up from anything he had achieved in his high school travels to date. What really drew Joe to Templeton, though, were his friends, three of whom stood out.

Naz Russo was a young man who looked mature beyond his years, with jet-black hair, menacing dark eyes and a five o'clock shadow that was a regular part of his appearance. Johnny Cucca, one of two boys and two girls in a family highly regarded at the school, had a smile that got him through all kinds of scrapes. When the smile failed him, his legendary temper and fighting style kicked in. With Johnny, you were never quite sure which would come first. The third member of the group was Andy, the gregarious friend Joe had met at Gladstone Secondary and who followed Joe's circuitous route to Templeton.

"The boys," as they were known, were infamous schoolwide for the blue '66 Chevy II they emptied out of every morning before the start of school. They spent lunch hours and breaks at school emulating professional wrestlers. Naz and Joe prided themselves on being the featured combatants, attracting a group of fascinated observers. Joe would leap from an imaginary turnbuckle, impersonating the famous Stampede grappler Dynamite Kid. Naz would absorb Joe's punishing blows and deliver a few of his own as Davey Boy Smith, the ferocious bull dog whose compass knew only one setting: straight ahead. The students who gathered around, fascinated by the craziness of these two, kept a respectful distance to make sure they didn't end up accidentally receiving a smash to the chops or a knee to the mid-section. When the teacher on hallway supervision approached the congested area, the match would come to an unceremonious halt, resuming once again once the teacher moved on. Johnny Cucca was not one for the fake Stampede fights, though, Joe recalls.

———

Cucca went from zero to three thousand mph in a heartbeat. He would spit on you and rip your eyes out if he had to; that was just the way he was wired. With Naz and me, there was an in-between, even a stop button. Not for Johnny. That's probably why he didn't participate in the Stampede stuff. He was afraid of what he might do.

Me and Andy with Naz, Albert, Steve, Mike, Marcello, various guys—you know, the Clark Parkers, the Riley Park Gang, the Italians (we had a couple of Chinese guys and a couple of Portuguese guys with us as well, though mostly they were part of the Clark Park Gang)—nearly went at it a couple of times at pre-grads. The pre-grads started early in our Grade 12 year and took place every single weekend. Fortunately, we never had it out on those occasions, but we certainly came close.

As for other Temp students, there were the Napier Boys—we called them the Disco Boys—guys who were good guys but were

connected to school in a much more positive way than we were. I
remember my dad telling me, "You wait, Joe; how much will you
like it when you are getting up at 6 a.m. going to a factory job
while they sleep in and work in the white-collar world of man-
agement? These are the guys who are going to be your bosses!"

Sure enough, I did end up later with a job at Nelson's Linen, a
stinky factory job where I went to work at six every morning and
basically just wanted to puke my lungs out—every single day.

Outside school, Joe's weeks were characterized by a plethora of
brawls, usually with combatants from just across the city bor-
der in the municipality of Burnaby. Coincidentally, Joe's uncle
Pietro served in that municipality as a respected school board
trustee before his political career took flight as a member of the
provincial legislature.

Every Friday at Templeton, it seemed, Joe would visit the
counsellor's office at the non-negotiable invitation of Gary Little. "Make this weekend the start of something totally different,
Joe," Little would admonish the teenager. "I don't want to see
you and Cucca come into the school on Monday morning with
the evidence of fighting all over your faces—cuts and black
eyes—or on your fists either. Try it just this once. If you could
make the kind of commitment to your studies that you do to
your fighting, you would probably crack the honour roll. That's
the kind of potential you have, Joe."

"Not to worry, sir. This weekend is when I start to pour the
coals to the books." With that, Joe would sally forth, a huge grin
on his unshaven face.

The results never varied. Joe, Andy, Johnny, Naz and their
cronies would meet up with another group, somewhere, somehow, and the brawl would be on.

One of the most memorable of these occurred just outside
Templeton. A group of students of Italian heritage—not Joe or
his gang, ironically enough—had got into an earlier altercation

with a group of students of Vietnamese ancestry. The "Viets," as they were known, were kids whose families had survived some of the harshest conditions of war, and then the marginally better conditions of refugee camps, which for many had followed the war's end before their emigration to Canada. These kids were not about to take crap from anyone, Italians or otherwise.

So when they decided that a student named Angelo had disrespected them, they came armed and ready to do battle. Trouble was they got the wrong kid and pounced on Joe's best friend, Andy.

Andy and I were walking down the road. Suddenly, I felt something on my shoulder. I turned around, and there were a bunch of these Vietnamese guys jumping around, threatening us and trying to stab us.

Andy was the first to remove his belt, swinging it wildly and connecting with the forehead of one of the attackers. I took off my Harley belt and held it in one hand. I took off my jean jacket in a swift, fluid motion and held it in the other. When one of them came at me with a knife, I swung the belt as hard as I could and cracked him square in the head with the buckle. The sound was sickening, like cracking a not-yet-ripe pumpkin with your fist. After collecting himself, the guy doubled back, this time on Andy.

I ran to a nearby picket fence and began ripping pickets off it in order to protect ourselves. I looked back, but already it was too late. Andy had been stabbed in the back.

With Andy bleeding in the nurse's office, a group of us—me, Albert, Pat, Marcello and Rino—found Andy's attackers in the Templeton Pool area. Albert and I went after everybody, even going so far as to hurl a full Coke machine at them. We were beyond out of control.

Not surprisingly, this episode—"melee" would be a better word—just about cost Joe and friends a chance at graduation.

Don McIntyre, one of the school's vice-principals and himself a product of Vancouver's east side, called them all together. Joe remembers the meeting.

Mr. McIntyre read us the riot act. Basically, he told us that if we ever did anything of the sort again, we would all be tossed from the school—I believe his words were "kicked to the curb"—and would not be allowed to graduate from another high school in Vancouver. To this day, I don't know if he had the power to do all that, but none of us were about to take any chances. He was royally pissed.

Another memorable incident erupted in Richmond, a suburb south of Vancouver and home to a junior football team called the Raiders. Joe's brother, Ralph, was a student at Gladstone Secondary. A member of the Clark Parkers, Ralph knew he could always count on Joe's support—and vice versa. So it was predictable that when Ralph was the recipient of a vicious crowbar attack to the back of his head—by a couple of Raiders, he thought—Joe rallied his friends to seek revenge.

Eighteen stitches—that's what Ralph ended up with. Eighteen stitches! I got together members of an Asian gang as well as the Clark Parkers and the Italians. We went to Richmond and rolled in with about sixty guys.

My brother and I kept trying to find the Raiders football team. Everywhere we stopped, we asked people if they knew where the Raiders were having their party. If we didn't get the right answer, we just destroyed the place and kept on going. Finally, we found the Raiders on a beach near No. 2 Road, where they were having a bonfire and slamming back a few beers.

Ralph and I, together with a guy who was one of the leaders of the Clark Parkers, walked down the embankment and right

*into the middle of this football team, who sat there kind of dis-
believing. What was going on? Who were these idiots who had
come to crash their party?*

*I walked up to the biggest one of them all, looked him square
in the eye and, gesturing with a sweep of my hand toward Ralph,
said to my brother, "Do you remember this guy?"*

*What this Raider and the rest of them didn't know was that
we had close to sixty guys positioned in hiding on the embankment. They were ready to pounce at a moment's notice. What
the Raiders also didn't know was that several of the embankment guys were seriously armed—guns, knives, bats, you name
it. Now, that was not our style; we were old school, just our fists
and our fighting skills. That's the way it was. You might have
got hurt, but you did not get killed. But these guys we brought
along thought differently. They had more firepower than some
regiments in the Canadian military.*

*The big guy sized me up. I'm sure he was thinking, "Who is
this punk, all 160 pounds of him?" As he drew close and before
Ralph even had a chance to answer my question, I whistled
loudly and the embankment came alive with bodies rushing
down it. It was like the cavalry coming across the hilltop in one
of those old cowboy movies, absolutely breathtaking.*

*The brawl was on, and what a brawl it was. I ended up
taking twenty-eight stitches to my hand, thanks to an errant
swing of a metal bar from one of my own guys. It didn't take
long for us to take care of business. The fight was over quickly.
Let's just say, when we first arrived, they were the Richmond
Raiders. When we left, they were the Richmond Runners. They
scattered everywhere.*

Every Monday, almost without fail, counsellor Gary Little would
again direct Joe into his office. The Monday following the Richmond brawl was no exception.

"Get the fuck into my office," Joe recalls Little saying on one exasperated occasion. Little steadfastly maintains he would never have used language of that type in a professional context. But his frustration with this kid, a kid he sincerely liked and wanted to help in the worst way possible, did boil over at times. "Unless you're training to be a prize fighter, or more likely just another two-bit street fighter, you're going nowhere except to an early grave," Little admonished. As always, Joe smiled and breezily committed to maintaining the peace.

As always, he had no intention of doing so.

JOE LOOKS BACK on those days with a kind of reverence, feelings we reserve for the special times in our lives. What was especially important for him were his relationships with Andy Amoroso, his best friend, and with Naz Russo, a friendship so deep and compelling that for Joe it was truly unconditional.

———

With Naz, these crazy things would happen. One time, on Nanaimo Street, we were street racing a guy named De Luca. Pedal to the metal, we were flying from Charles Street up the hill heading south. Suddenly, a car comes out of a side street. I had to gear down while simultaneously slamming on the brakes. I have a four-speed stick in the car, so I drop it into third and try to slam it into second. At that point, I totally lose control. Totally. Corvettes do that. They will spin out on you fairly easily. Something to do with too much torque combined with too light a rear end.

I am now doing 360s down Nanaimo Street, totally out of control—and on the wrong side of the street. Suddenly, another car comes out and cuts me off. I do everything I can to avoid it, but keep in mind that I am still doing 360s and fighting for control of the vehicle. Somehow, I miss that car and spin to a halt eighteen inches from a parked car.

I slap the stick shift back into second and resume driving. Adrenalin about to rupture my veins, I look over at Naz, who by now is totally white-knuckled, his hands gripping the dash like he's trying to choke the life out of it. He looks right back at me and starts screaming at the top of his lungs. That was probably the first time he questioned our friendship.

Then there was the time that Naz and I were at Coconuts [a Vancouver nightclub] on Kingsway Avenue. I get into a fight and end up in jail. Somehow the keys to my dad's car had fallen out in the chaos. Naz finds them, takes Dad's Chevrolet Cavalier and promptly drives it right into a wall. Straight into it—can you believe it? Trouble is he doesn't tell me. Probably too drunk to think it all through. I have to phone Dad from the jail and let him know where I am and why. Dad doesn't believe me at first. On top of that, he wonders where the hell his car is.

"Don't worry," I say. "You'll get it back."

Dad finally got his car back, all right, but not as it was when it left the house. Thanks to Naz, it was totally smashed—thanks to Naz himself being totally smashed.

———

In addition to alcohol, drugs played a growing part in Joe's life, beginning in Grade 8. By Grade 10 he was using cocaine and marijuana, along with an array of hallucinogens: magic mushrooms, acid, whatever was available and could be ingested. This was a portent of what would come later in Joe's life, when drugs—particularly cocaine—just about ended it.

Joe's high school career continued. Joe at this point could best be described as scraping by, doing enough to avoid the fate that had befallen him on his stops elsewhere, but only by the thinnest of margins. His relationship with Jim Crescenzo made a difference, though Templeton's drama teacher wondered at times if Joe would ever learn to play by the rules.

———

Jim had me in his program so that he could keep an eye on me. Toward this end, he would take me on tour with the theatre group, working backstage and helping in any way I could.

This happened twice. Sure enough, brawls broke out and—
surprise, surprise—I wasn't allowed on the tours anymore.

There was, however, a positive that came from all of this. I got
to work as an extra on Rocky IV, *which was being filmed in Van-*
couver. I even have the shorts to prove it, along with a picture
from the Province *newspaper. I guess I looked like Rocky at the*
time. That's undoubtedly how I landed the nickname Little Rocky.

––––––––

Despite the setbacks, Joe eventually earned his diploma, something that at one time had seemed unattainable, certainly to
most of his teachers. Joe had done the impossible. He had completed Grade 12.

In school and out of it, his friendships with Andy, Naz, Cucca
and the rest of the boys continued unabated. Fast cars. Fast
girls. Fast fists. All this coupled with alcohol and drugs. The
formula never seemed to change. What did change were their
conversations. Increasingly, their thoughts turned to death,
particularly for Naz, who felt, deep in his soul, that his life was
not to be a long one.

––––––––

In retrospect, my conversations at the time with Naz remind
me of my relationship with Donny Roming. Donny used to say
that he would not live to see forty. Turned out he was right—
well, almost right. He was killed a couple of months short of his
forty-first birthday.

Naz was similar. He somehow knew death was coming at him
fast and early in his life. Maybe it was the near misses he had
had along the way. Maybe that's why he got married at such a
young age. Or maybe it was simply the feeling he had within him,
a kind of message from a higher power. We talked about it quite
a bit. That sense of death definitely affected how he lived his life.

One time, Naz and Cucca were up in Osoyoos, a picturesque
lake town in the BC *Interior dotted by vineyards and orchards.*

Cucca had a beautiful 454 baby-blue Corvette, a head-turning car that was his pride and joy. They sped along a narrow asphalt road, a slight sheen of mist covering it, which meant slippery conditions, especially in a 'Vette, which I had previously learned the hard way has way too much rear-end torque for anything but the driest of conditions. Sure enough, they ended up spinning out of control. The car was a total wreck, but both Johnny and Naz survived without any serious injuries.

For Joe, as for Andy, Naz and Johnny, the end of high school meant the start of the next chapter in life. But what would those new chapters bring? As Joe headed out into the world, his diploma under his belt, he wasn't quite sure.

4

I F Joe's friends were worried his entry into the adult world of work would change his life or his personality, they need not have been.

True, Joe got a responsible job. He performed it faithfully, even though he could barely stand it. Nelson's Linen and Laundry, the same place his mother worked, was his new place of employment.

———

The shifts were long, and I soon realized that this was not my thing. The place was stinky; furthermore, I had to be up at 6 a.m. in order to get to work on time. Hardly what a guy my age wants, especially a guy who enjoys the nightlife. This was exactly what my dad had warned me about. But I did stay with it for two full years. If nothing else, you cannot say that I am a quitter.

———

Joe left his job at Nelson's Linen and Laundry in order to attend the British Columbia Institute of Technology, or BCIT, a diploma-and-degree-granting institution located in central Burnaby. He enrolled in the Business Department, from which he obtained his diploma in relatively short order. Sure enough, when motivated, Joe had what it took to succeed as a student, something that had eluded him to that point in his life.

Upon graduation from BCIT, Joe applied for and got a job at A&B Sound—known locally as simply A&B—one of Vancouver's premier outlets specializing in car stereos, vinyl records, cassette tapes and CDs. The job allowed him to combine his sales and marketing acumen with his love of audio equipment for cars. The match was a good one. After a year on the floor as a salesman, Joe was promoted to manager and soon was placed in charge of the prestigious Seymour Street location, A&B's flagship store.

During his four years at the Seymour Street store, Joe impressed his superiors with his product knowledge, salesmanship and leadership skills. When a purchasing position became available, he knew that he was ready for it and would excel at it. Unfortunately, the job went to another employee who had been with the company for ten years. There is no doubt seniority played a major part in the final selection, but that was it for Joe. Never one to accept losing easily—particularly in cases such as this, where he knew he was the more qualified for the position—he decided to part company with A&B.

Following this disappointment, life for Joe became reminiscent of his earlier days. He hit Vancouver's top nightclubs on a regular basis, his favourite being Richard's on Richards, known affectionately to locals as Dick's on Dicks. Characterized by its thumping bass beats peppering eminently forgettable dance tunes, web-like laser shows and abundant chrome and metal surroundings, Richard's on Richards was the place to see and be seen.

Joe fit right in. He cut an impressive figure, his stylishly long black hair falling casually to the starched white collar barely visible above a dark and fashionable Italian jacket, his posture confident and poised. His eyes were drawn to two elements at the club: girls he hoped to make out with later that evening, and guys who might be willing to fight him right then and there. Joe's reputation on both fronts continued to grow.

Like his dad years earlier, Joe also vowed that from now on he would be his own boss. At A&B he had specialized in cellular phones, becoming the company's number-one cell phone salesman in short order. So it wasn't surprising when he decided to open his own "store"—a mobile one at that—run out of the trunk of his car.

His beginnings were modest. His automobile served not only as his retail outlet but also as his office. A friend who worked for the Save-On-Foods grocery chain agreed to be Joe's silent partner. When Joe asked the friend how he could afford to invest in something that would, initially at least, pay so little, the friend laughed. "Easy, bro," he said. "Where I work I get paid to stock shelves and help old ladies to their cars with carts full of groceries. As far as supporting you and your business, I sell cigarettes on the side."

"Sell cigarettes?" Joe queried. "Tell me how that works."

"No problemo," the friend said. "I steal 'em and then sell 'em at discounts to fences and friends, anyone I can trust to keep his mouth shut. The beauty is it's all profit, and the profit is all mine. So, you see, I can work with you for very little or even no return, as long as my retail cigarette business continues to flourish."

Joe was intrigued. This was the type of partner he was thrilled to find, as well as an example of the type of business he wished he had, all profit and no overhead. He didn't want to serve time for stealing the product, however. He'd seen what jail had done to his dad, and given his own brief stints spent behind bars, he was determined it would never happen to him on any kind of long-term basis.

Joe expanded his business, doing what he considered the next best thing to selling contraband cigarettes. It was not a lofty 100 percent return on product, but a solid if modest 7 percent. He obtained a licence from Telus, the largest phone company in the province. For the better part of the twentieth century, BC Tel, as the company had previously been known, had the monopoly on phone service in British Columbia. The year was 1993.

At the time, you could earn a $200 commission for selling a cell phone together with the Telus package. The best part was that 7 percent of the client's monthly cell phone bill was paid directly to me. By then, I had opened a small office on Kingsway Avenue, but I still had next to no overhead—the rent alone was only $300 per month. I was off and running.

Now that he was no longer working out of the trunk of his car, Joe was able to design the interior of his retail outlet. His palette of colours and use of space were ahead of their time—so far ahead, in fact, that his design ideas were utilized by Telus for many of its stores. As a budding entrepreneur, Joe was also careful to leave himself some free time.

Mondays to Fridays were spent growing the business. Friday nights, Saturdays and even Sundays were my time—time for partying, time for going to clubs with friends.

During this period, an important encounter took place. One day a Chinese-Canadian man walked into Joe's office. "I'd like to buy a cell phone," the man mumbled.

There was something sinister about the guy, Joe thought. Maybe it was the black trench coat he wore. Maybe it was the fact that he failed to remove his sunglasses, even though he was inside a store where not a ray of sunshine found entry. Then again, it might have been his slicked-back hair, an overall look that to Joe smacked of gang involvement.

It didn't take long for Joe to sell the guy a phone and the lucrative Telus package that went with it.

"My name is Joe," Joe told the man. "If there's anything else I can do, don't hesitate to give me a call. I'm here to help."

"Thanks, man. My name is Nez," said the customer. "N-E-Z. Pleased to meet you, Joe."

Once the sale was completed, Joe and Nez continued to chat. Not about phones this time, but about gangs and martial arts, things that were near and dear to Joe's heart. They also chatted about Joe's plans to open another store. That was it, or so Joe expected, as Nez exited the building. "Good guy. I like that guy," Joe thought.

The next day, Nez returned. He walked quietly into the store, holding a cardboard box in front of him.

"Nez, good to see you. What's up, man? Didn't the phone work out?" Joe asked.

"No, the phone is fine—no problem. I came to set this thing up," said Nez, pointing to the box. "I've come to work for you. I've brought you a computer."

"What the hell?" Joe responded. "There's no way I can afford to pay you, and I don't even know what you propose to do with that damn computer. It's not like I need it, especially this early in my business."

"Don't worry," Nez reassured him. "I'll set up all your business systems on it and bring your store into the twentieth century. Everyone is using computers these days for accounting, databases, marketing materials—pretty much everything."

"You don't get it," Joe countered. "Nez, I can't afford you, and I can't afford the machine, much as I would love to. I can't even consider your offer. Not a penny, not a nickel, not a dime. Nothing. Get it?"

"Not to worry," said Nez. "Pay me later. I see something in you I like, Joe. I know you'll be able to pay me someday—and pay me well. Someday. Guaranteed."

Joe didn't continue to say no. How could he?

For the next three years, Nez worked for the business like a man possessed. Three solid years, and during that time he did not earn a single penny from working for Joe. Yet he never uttered a complaint.

The business flourished. Joe opened his second store at the corner of Nanaimo and Hastings Streets, mere blocks from Templeton Secondary. A short time later, he opened a third store a mile or so east, on Hastings at Boundary Road, in Burnaby. There was a high volume of traffic at this new location, and Joe's already booming business boomed even more.

When the third store opened, Joe appointed the one person he knew would be the hardest-working, most trustworthy general manager he could imagine: Nez, the indomitable friend who had given three years of his life free of charge to help Joe get his business established.

————

Nez became my highest-paid employee as payment for all his hard work and dedication. I eventually expanded to two other locations, one store going into Kamloops, the other into Cloverdale [a section of Surrey, the sprawling suburb east of Vancouver]. At this point we were making money. Lots of money. Life was good.

————

While things were good for Joe's business, his personal life was careening out of control. Still only twenty-five years of age, he continued to frequent nightclubs and to do the one thing that gave him the kind of respect he coveted, something even his business enterprise did not seem to bring: he fought. Not just occasionally or because he had been wronged, but frequently and for no reason at all other than the love of it.

Throughout British Columbia's Lower Mainland, Joe's reputation continued to grow. He was known as a shit disturber, somebody who not only incited mayhem with talk but backed it up with his actions. No longer the kid who had been bullied at Lord Selkirk, Joe was on the constant prowl for foes he could turn into victims of his own.

His own sphere of influence expanded as it intersected with others. There was Turk, an acquaintance from one of the many high schools Joe had attended. Their mothers worked together, which meant right from the start they had that in common. There was Angelo, a crazy character if ever there was one, a guy Joe met one evening—where else—at a club in town. They too clicked immediately.

As it turned out, Joe's new friend Angelo was a full-patch member of the Hells Angels. Turk was Angelo's hang-around, a kind of apprentice. Joe looked up to both of them, but particularly to Angelo. He admired the way people cleared a path for Angelo when he entered a room. He admired the way women were drawn to Angelo, attracted to the bad-boy persona that was part and parcel of the lifestyle. He admired the way other guys did not mess with Angelo. Ever.

From that moment forward, Joe knew what he wanted.

His mind kept returning to a conversation he had held with Naz Russo before Naz's untimely death in 1995. "Joe, I know what I want to do with my life. I want to become a full-patch member of the H.A."

At the time, Joe had looked incredulously at his buddy. Sure, he and Naz lived life on the edge, but they were certainly nowhere close to being in the same league as the Angelos or Turks of the world. But Naz wouldn't let it go. "I may never get there, Joe, but I will certainly do my best."

Joe had sat speechless, a cauldron of conflicting responses. He could not believe what he was hearing from his friend. On the other hand, he pledged to himself that if Naz was unable to achieve his goal, he would step in and fulfill it for him.

Naz had been a passenger in his friend Enzo's truck when the vehicle slammed into a hydro pole, shearing the pole in two.

Miraculously, Enzo and two other passengers, Gerry Zaccardi and Ray Abraham, survived. One did not. Naz's nine lives were up. He died at the scene, leaving behind a grieving young wife and a stunned and grieving group of friends.

Joe took the loss hard. He admits today that Naz's death had consequences he could never have envisioned at the time. There was the incredible sense of emptiness that death triggers and also, thrown into bold relief, the commitment he'd secretly made to his best friend: to fulfill Naz's dream of becoming a full-patch Hells Angel. Now Joe's chance to do that had come. He decided to take the plunge.

ONE NIGHT A number of Hells Angels, accompanied by two or three aspirants to the patch, including Joe, made their way from their East Vancouver clubhouse to Richard's on Richards, where they found Angelo, a full-patch member, deep into his cognac. That much Joe knew for sure, though what else Angelo might have ingested, Joe couldn't say. Angelo was unpredictable at the best of times, Joe knew, and when he was in this state, trouble was quick to follow.

At a certain point, Angelo laid his eyes on an African-Canadian man whose physical presence seemed to dominate the club. At least six foot five and well over three hundred pounds, the man looked like Goliath in a room full of Davids. The more Angelo drank, the more he fixed his attention on the man. Without provocation and with absolutely no warning, Angelo sprang to his feet. The vast quantity of alcohol he had consumed had not impaired his physical prowess. He rushed headlong at the behemoth and began throwing punches, kicking recklessly, even attempting a head-butt: whatever might give him an advantage in a fight where he appeared to be hopelessly outmatched.

Angelo also had the benefit of his hang-arounds, who were obligated to protect him. Two or three of them jumped into the fracas as well. The moment they did, the advantage shifted quickly from the big man to Angelo.

The tall man, now enraged, extricated himself from the mass of flailing bodies. "That's it, you mother-fuckers," he screamed over the din of the music. "You're all going to pay. I'm coming back at you with my gun." With that, he made a beeline for his car, parked just outside the club.

Joe grabbed at Angelo. "Let's go, man, we've got to get out of here. Now!" With difficulty, Joe wrestled Angelo down the stairs and out of the club. The moment they hit the chill of the night air, they knew they were in trouble.

"Mother-fucker" they heard someone yell from directly behind them. Angelo jumped into a slow-moving car. With a squeal of burning rubber he was gone, leaving his hang-arounds behind. Joe ran for cover into a nearby parking lot. The *pop-pop-pop* of gunfire followed him. Some of the bullets slammed into the bodies of cars; others bounced off, the metallic ping ringing in Joe's ears. More bullets strafed the asphalt of the parking lot.

Stranded perilously close to the shooter, Joe moved stealthily behind a couple of parked vehicles shrouded in the shadows of a low-rise building. He remained as quiet as he could, even as he hyperventilated and fought for his breath.

"One, two, three . . ." Joe counted the shots as they emptied from the man's gun. When the total had reached eighteen, he felt certain that the clip was empty and made his run for safety. Either he had guessed right or the man had decided he'd had enough. The gunfire ceased.

On Joe's circuitous route back to the clubhouse, his mind was in overdrive. He worried that Angelo might have been hit, even fatally shot. He was worried that one of his other bros might have been hit as well. The thought even crossed his mind that someone totally innocent might have taken a bullet. And for what? He tried his cell phone but was unable to get so much as a dial tone. The irony of the situation was not lost on him.

Finally, he arrived back at the H.A. house. He pressed the buzzer to gain entry—not with the panic of someone who needed help but with the indifference of someone who had minor business to conduct. The door swung open. Angelo, a glass of coppery cognac in hand, stood there laughing heartily and demanding of Joe, "Where the hell have you been, bro?" He directed Joe inside and calmly closed the door behind him.

"Looks like you need one too, bro!" Angelo suggested, reaching for another glass. There was not a hint of worry in his demeanour. For all anyone observing the scene might have guessed, Angelo had been at the house all evening playing a low-stakes game of Texas hold 'em. Joe was disbelieving. Here was a guy who had just been shot at, and he was laughing as if he had spent the last two hours at a George Carlin concert. Joe knew in that instant that the H.A. clubhouse was the right place for him.

———

I began hanging out with the guys in the club more often. They started coming to the store, and we were hanging out together on weekends. I started to desire the lifestyle. People look at the patch and see power and the glory. It puts you on a pedestal. It's like being a rock star. No matter what age, young or old, people always take notice when a member walks into a room. Whether they admit it or not, people like the badass. I know that from first-hand experience. When you walk into that environment, you walk in as a movie star might stride onto a set.

———

Badasses weren't welcome everywhere, though, and one day Joe's boss at Telus asked Joe to stop by his office.

"Joe," he began, "there's something we need to talk about. You've been under police surveillance for a while now. I'm sure you know that. The guys you're hanging out with are not exactly conducive to the Telus brand. Let me be straight. You have some hard choices to make: sell the business or give up your new-found friends."

It didn't take Joe long to make up his mind. Businesses came and went. True friends were with you for life. He got well over six figures for his business, a considerable sum in those days, especially for a guy most people thought would never make it through high school. He had money in his pocket now, and a new goal to pursue.

5

LIFE in the Calendino household continued like it always had. Nerina and Frank supported their family through a combination of hard work and abiding love. Joe was the oldest of the children—a son at that—and as such enjoyed a place of prominence in the sibling hierarchy, as was the case in many Italian families. However, it was clear to Joe's family as well as his friends that he was starting to move in a different direction. For one thing, the cell phone business that had once seemed so promising was now officially a thing of the past. For another, the people he associated with had changed; familiar faces were replaced by faces his family and old friends did not recognize.

Ralph, Joe's younger brother by one year, minded his own business. What Joe was up to was Joe's concern; what Ralph was involved with was Ralph's concern. Plain and simple. Furthermore, Ralph was on a career trajectory he did not want compromised by the behaviour of his beloved older brother. The less he knew about Joe's dealings the better. Nonetheless, Frank's admonitions about "family thick or thin, through good times and bad" were as deeply ingrained in Ralph as they were in his elder sibling.

Eva, the youngest by five years, was not the pampered youngest child found in some families. She was rock-solid, a hard worker. Along with her brothers, she helped out in the family's janitorial business, and she continued to cook the family dinners on school nights.

The three children had all been baptized, though none had been confirmed or taken their First Communion. Nonetheless, while they were growing up, Nerina insisted that the children say a prayer at bedtime, a habit that was part of her upbringing and one that brought a measure of comfort and calm at the end of what were often demanding days. When the boys reached their teens, they revolted against this practice, and Nerina didn't think it worth the effort to press the point. There were more important things to worry about.

While the family often struggled economically, they enjoyed good times. Many friends and relatives graced the Calendino home, a welcoming place redolent with smells of sausage, simmering pasta sauces and fermenting homemade wine accompanied by traditional Italian songs played at high volume.

"I don't want your friends to feel they have to go elsewhere," Frank told his kids. "They are always welcome here. Better you have a few drinks under our roof than sneak around and get into trouble somewhere else." His attitude and warmth enveloped even Joe's burgeoning group of new friends.

Mom was known as Mrs. C., while everyone called Dad "Pops" or Mr. C. Our home was open twenty-four hours a day. The original 7-Eleven. I don't even think we locked the doors back then.

Over the years, as they could afford it, Frank and Nerina updated the house. The original green carpet was torn out and replaced with beautiful Italian terrazzo tile. The basement, affectionately known among the kids as the Dungeon, was transformed into a combination basement suite, wine cellar and laundry room. The suite had been off limits to the children when they were very young—it was rented out to provide the family with an additional revenue stream—but the Dungeon had become a popular gathering spot for one and all as Joe, Ralph and then Eva entered their teen years.

Joe and Ralph shared a room, a typical arrangement for kids growing up in multi-child families. What was not typical was that the boys' bedroom doubled as Joe's drum studio. Ralph, for his part, blasted away on the trumpet or sax. Eva kept down the decibel level in the house by focusing on the clarinet for a short time. Then, not to be outdone by her brothers, she switched to the drums, trombone and sax, instruments that would not get lost in the cacophony of the Calendino household.

The family routine of work, work and more work as a group had come to a halt in 1991. That was the year the kids, who had all finished high school by then, decided to get on with their own lives. Joe had always been the protector, the tough one of the three. Ralph was the compassionate middle child, and Eva was the "baby"—and the lone girl in the family. Frank and Nerina gave their two boys vast freedom whereas Eva was kept on what she calls a "short rope."

Once they reached adulthood, not a whole lot changed. The three siblings continued to live in the family home. Joe remained the tough guy, interested in proving to the world he'd do whatever it took to pummel his foes into submission. Ralph mixed compassion with determination to succeed in the topsy-turvy world of Vancouver's construction business. Eva advanced her career working in the laundry business at the same time as she dated and eventually fell deeply in love with Nick, the man who one day would become her husband.

Anchoring it all were Nerina and Frank. They loved their kids and stood by them through life's vicissitudes. Frank knew what it meant to be separated from his family, to spend hard time in British Columbia's harshest jail. He vowed he would never turn his back on family or friends, the way some people had turned their backs on him during the darkest period of his life, the time he considered to be his period of greatest need.

FROM AN EARLY age, Joe believed he was destined for success. No matter how hard his parents worked to keep the family solvent, Joe knew there were better times ahead, for them and for him. He was convinced he would be better off materially than his folks were, and that others would respect him for who he was and what he had become in life.

During his high school years, Joe comported himself with the kind of confidence only someone with a deep belief in himself possesses. He was respectful to teachers and administrators. He was polite, even deferential, to cafeteria staff and custodial workers. He was fair-minded. If he did something wrong, he accepted the consequences. If he was unjustly accused, he fought with every fibre of his being to prove his accuser wrong.

Joe was born to be a leader, and his views on leadership were as unadorned as his personality. Hard work and determination were a central part of the equation. Being loyal and expecting loyalty from his peers meant as much to Joe as either of these attributes; loyalty was the foundation of successful leadership, as Joe viewed it. Also crucial to his street-based upbringing was the view that others would try to impose boundaries on you. Your job, if you were to succeed in life, was to smash through those boundaries to prove these people wrong.

While there are those who say Joe lived for trouble, there are others who state with equal conviction that he never initiated a fight—though this latter group is decidedly in the minority. According to them, Joe fought only when provoked. His sister, Eva, emphatically affirms this. "Never," she says. "Joe would never start a fight, but he would never back down either. In fact, after he had kicked their ass, he felt terrible. As tough as he was ..." Her words fade into silence, the unspoken message being that beneath Joe's hard exterior is a man of deep feeling, something that in the early days only those close to him could know.

Joe was constantly surrounded by friends and acquaintances who looked up to him. He'd made good money in his thriving cell phone business. He had a caring and supportive family, and his good looks were a carbon copy of his father's. He was rarely without a girlfriend, sometimes several, a pattern that was to repeat itself through most of his adult life. So why did a young man with so much going for him decide he would risk it all for "the lifestyle"? The answer was simple. He had made it his goal.

A process of studied deliberation was not Joe's modus operandi. He made the decision to strive for membership in the Hells Angels brashly, almost impetuously, relying on instinct rather than analysis. His obligation to Naz played a significant role. In his mind, Joe had made a commitment to his friend; he would honour that commitment. But there was something else at play. Joe wanted more in life, and he was convinced that being a full-patch member of such a prestigious group—as he saw it—would provide that.

———

Being a Hells Angel is a niche commodity. Not many people wear a patch. It always grabs attention. I wanted a piece of that.

———

Joe did not set his sights at entry or mid-level either. Not at all. If he was going down this road, he wanted in at the highest level possible—as a charter member of the Nomads, the elite of the H.A. elite. To achieve that, Joe knew he would need guidance, the wise and firm hand of somebody who knew the ropes from A to Z. That person, his H.A. sponsor, turned out to be Donny Roming.

6

FATE connected Joe and Donny Roming twenty years after their first encounter—at the infamous party in Vancouver's East End. When their paths crossed again, Donny decided to take Joe under his wing. One thing he modelled for Joe was the importance of loyalty and respect.

———

I spent days on end with this man, and he showed me nothing but respect. I loved him as a brother loves another brother. He had the looks of a Hulk Hogan and the mischievous personality of a Jim Carrey, a smile that was almost perpetually pasted to his face. Women were drawn to him like pins to a magnet— woman after woman, all types, all ages. I will miss him and our friendship forever.

———

Public accounts of Donny Roming speak to other aspects of his character. There's the Grade 9 photo of him posted alongside his inscription on the "Classmate Profiles" section for Eric Hamber Secondary School:

May 17, 1960–March 9, 2001: Donny was fatally shot outside a Yaletown bar following a dispute. Donny was a member of the Nomads chapter of the Hells Angels.

"As we lay ourselves to sleep
We pray to God your soul to keep
To guide us safely through our day
In our hearts is where you'll stay
We miss you, Daddy"

Cole and Angelina (in memoriam, *The Province*, March 10, 2002)

Looking at that picture of Donny, a fresh-faced, blond fourteen-year-old, one would be hard-pressed to imagine what lay ahead for him.

———

One night Donny and I ended up at an after-hours club. At the time, he had a running feud going with a guy I'll call Justin, a guy he had a serious hate-on for. Now, Donny had been without sleep for three nights straight. Booze. Drugs. Anything to keep the party going.

So we're in this club when, through the haze of cigarette smoke, Donny spots Justin. "That piece of shit," he says. He leaps to his feet and races to where Justin is sitting. The next thing I know, Donny has Justin pinned against a wall and is laying a serious beating on him. Lefts. Rights. He was beside himself with anger, and it showed in every punch he threw. I rushed over to where all this was going on.

"Joe," Donny screams at me. "Shoot this piece of shit. Shoot him. I want you to kill him—now!"

I wedged myself between the two combatants, grabbed Justin by the shirt and threw him through the front doors of the club onto the street. Justin made his getaway, slowly at first and then remarkably fast for a man who had just been pummeled. Could I have shot him? Sure. Did I shoot him? No. The answer is simple. I knew Justin from Vancouver's east side. Not really a bad guy, but he had crossed Donny. Big mistake. But I just let him go.

Back inside the club, I sat down with Donny, who was now totally relaxed and nursing a beer. "Did you shoot him, Joe?" he asked.

"No," I said. "He got away."

"Okay." And with that, he calmly finished his drink.

————————

While Donny may have looked like a cherubic choirboy in his ninth-grade picture, he was anything but that in his adult life. The man Joe revered was a serious badass. But that did not taint in any way the high regard Joe held for Donny. If anything, it heightened it. Donny was a Nomad, so not surprisingly, Joe's aspirations led him in the direction of the Nomads as well.

————————

This is the charter that I went for. The Nomads are one of the toughest charters to make. Out of twenty-eight guys, only three of us were successful.

————————

In what may be one of the most remarkable conversations a family has shared at a dinner table, Joe announced matter-of-factly to his family one evening, "I have something to tell you. I need you all to listen."

The room, normally ringing with top-volume, animated banter, went silent. Knowing Joe, the family hoped for the best but expected the worst, particularly given the changes of late in Joe's life. Something horrible has happened, thought Nerina and Frank. Frank leaned in to make sure he would hear every word.

"I'm going to become a Hells Angel." Joe's voice was soft, deliberate.

"*What?*" It was like an Italian chorus, with everybody responding as one.

"I said I'm going to become a Hells Angel."

No one said a word for what seemed an eternity. People studied the plates in front of them or looked elsewhere. Finally, Joe's dad pushed himself back in his chair. Laying down his knife and fork before clearing his throat, he responded, "Are you sure this is what you want to do with your life, son?"

"Yes, Dad, it's exactly what I want to do," Joe replied.

"Well," said Frank, "if that's what you want to do, become a Hells Angel, Joe, then do it."

Later, in conversation with Ralph and Eva, Frank defended his response. "What else was I going to say?" he asked them. "Joe knows we love him and that we will support him, whatever, wherever, whenever."

"Even if it's the Hells Angels?"

"Yes, even if it's the Hells Angels."

With his commitment now quite public, Joe was in "balls deep," as he describes it today. Anybody who doubted his resolve, who viewed his decision as a passing phase, was sadly mistaken. Failure was not an option.

The only person who openly challenged Joe was his sister, Eva. Unlike their father, she saw nothing but the downside in her brother's decision.

"I told Joe, these guys are like rookie cops," she recalls. "They get their badge and they think they're tough; they pull you over for no reason except now they can, legally. Take off that badge, take off the patch, and they're just an average joe. They're just like the rest of us."

Joe grimaced at being called an average joe, something he abhorred. Although he loved his sister, he was not about to be swayed by her unsolicited advice. "Then you don't really know who I am, Eva, do you? It's about respect."

Eva shook her head, frustrated at Joe's stubbornness. "Joe, what are you talking about? You have respect! You don't need this crap in order to get more."

In retrospect, Eva says she knew why he was doing it. "I knew his commitment to Naz, how Naz had walked into the office and told Joe he was going to become an Angel, how one week later Naz was killed in that senseless accident. Naz's plan became Joe's plan. He became obsessed with it. Furthermore, he had grown up on the east side of Vancouver with so many of these guys that he almost felt he was part of the group even before he decided to become part of the group. He had a head start."

Weeks after the dinner conversation at the Calendino house, Joe was asked by a full-patch member of the Nomads why he wanted to become one himself. Replying straight from the heart, as he always did, Joe said bluntly: "I want to be part of a brotherhood. I want to be with a group of guys who are willing to live and die for one another."

7

BRANDON Steele. The name sounds like it belongs in a piece of crime fiction. Make no mistake about it, though. Brandon Steele is a real person, as real as the spray of a shower turned full blast to cold. Like that spray, Brandon can be in your face with no prospect of warming, if necessary. He was certainly a cold slap in the face of Joe Calendino.

Neither a large man nor one given to hyperbole, Constable Steele of the Vancouver Police Department was not afraid of anyone or anything. At least, that was the appearance he gave.

A graduate of Simon Fraser University's Criminology Department, Constable Steele was as interested in the cognitive side of police work as he was in the adrenalin-pumping physical side. He believed the thin blue line was what separated a civilized society from an anarchic one. Consequently, his work was not merely about day-to-day skirmishes with gang members. He was motivated by a nobler purpose.

Since November 24, 1999, Brandon Steele has served the VPD in different roles. His seven and a half years in patrol were followed by assignment to the department's Missing Women Task

Force. Today, he carries the rank of detective constable in his role as school liaison officer for alternative schools in Vancouver.

On the night Donny Roming was murdered outside Bar None in Vancouver's Yaletown, Brandon Steele was one of the first officers on the scene. He and his partner were patrolling the downtown core at the time, and they responded immediately to the call of a shooting. From Steele's point of view, Donny's death represented one less gang member tearing up the streets of Vancouver. Good riddance.

A couple of nights later, the two police officers drove down Hamilton Street. Outside Bar None, a group of bikers had gathered. Their motorcycles were parked in neat 45-degree angles to the curb, chrome finishes reflecting prisms of colour. Brandon and his partner pulled up alongside. Even from the distance of their idling car, they could see the grief on every biker's face. A makeshift memorial had started to take shape: flowers, short notes, assorted memorabilia. Grown men who looked like they could tear someone apart limb by limb spilled tears unabashedly.

Suddenly, Brandon's partner rolled down the window of their police cruiser. Pretending he had a Kleenex clutched to his face, he looked out at the gathered throng. "Boo-hoo-hoo," he taunted. "I feel so bad for all of you. Boo-hoo. Poor little Donny."

Despite Joe not being part of the gathered throng, he soon heard all about it, as did everyone else in the club. No wonder he hated Brandon Steele and everyone associated with him.

JOE AND BRANDON harbour different memories of the night they first met, during the police response to a call about a disturbance in the heart of Vancouver's nightclub district. Upon arrival, the first thing Steele and his partner noticed was that the stanchions supporting the lineup ropes at the club in question had been knocked askew. The second thing they noticed was a doorman signalling them inside.

"We get out of our car. We cross the street, and two guys exit the bar," recalls Steele. "The guy I was working with taps one of them on the shoulder, and he turns around. I recognize him right away as a Hells Angel. It was Joe Calendino. He continues to walk westbound on Smithe Street, so I go right up to him, grab him by the shirt and start talking to him.

"At this point, I still really don't know what is going on, except that there has been a disturbance inside the club. Maybe there has been an assault; I really don't know. Joe turns to me and tries to minimize everything.

"'Hey,' says Joe, 'I am just leaving. Nothing going on here. I am out of here, man.'"

Steele tightened his grip on Joe and told him that he wasn't going anywhere, that Steele had some questions that needed to be answered. Again Joe protested.

"'I'm just leaving,' he says. 'I didn't do anything. Nothing. Am I under arrest or something? Come on, man. Just let me go.'

"At that point, I look over to where my partner is with the other member of the H.A. My partner is putting handcuffs on this individual, so I say to Joe, 'Why don't you put your hands behind your back and then we will sit down and sort all of this out?'"

When Joe refused to comply, Steele directed him toward a nearby wall and told Joe to put his hands behind his back.

"At this point," Steele recalls, "Joe is not fighting, but he certainly is not doing what I'm telling him to do. The situation is escalating."

When it became clear that Joe had no intention of complying with Constable Steele's orders, Steele attempted to take him to the ground.

"As I try to do so, I see that he has a loaded .45 calibre Glock in his waistband—tucked right in the back. That's when I realize why he doesn't want to turn around and have me handcuff him. The bloody guy is armed."

In the scuffle that ensued, Joe's gun fell from his waistband to the ground, sliding out of reach. "Gun, gun, gun!" Steele shouted, trying to alert both his partner and the two other officers who had by now arrived on the scene. Steele and Joe wrestled one another on the cold pavement of Smithe Street, Joe struggling to get away, Brandon equally determined to cuff him. The next thing Steele saw was a polished black shoe seemingly coming out of nowhere. It stomped down on the gun. One of the other officers had nabbed it.

"I got Joe by the wrist, pulling his other arm away from the gun, and I ended up breaking his wrist," Steele says. "After the big fight, I finally ended up getting him handcuffed. I was in a fight for my life. My sense was that if Joe had got to the gun, he would have used it."

At the time of this incident, Joe was not yet a Hells Angel, though Steele had identified him as one. He was merely a prospect trying to work his way into the club. Immediately after the handcuffs were finally slapped on Joe, two other bikers arrived. According to VPD report, one was a full-patch member of the club. The other, like Joe, was an associate. A fight broke out between these two newcomers and the police officers, and another gun went skidding across the pavement. It was clear to Steele and his fellow officers that these boys meant business.

"I think that incident really cemented the hate-fest that Joe had for me. He not only took quite a few shots in the fight—including a broken wrist—but also he was found guilty later on a firearm charge. That was really when I got to know who Joe Calendino was."

Joe, for his part, has a different recollection of their first encounter.

———

Of all the cops I came into contact with at that time in my life, the one I hated more than any other—and trust me, I hated 'em all—was Brandon Steele. I hated that guy. Full stop.

I have since come to respect Brandon and view him as a brother—call him the prodigal brother, if you will. I guess if I'm being truly honest, I am the prodigal brother. Either way, he and I have developed a deep and abiding respect for each other. That said, I will say without the least shadow of a doubt that the way Brandon has described that fight is total BS. *He's right, I did suffer an injury—but I never would have shot a cop, even if I had had the chance, ever. Even Brandon Steele, as much as I detested him at the time. I'll leave it at that.*

A later incident underscores further the animosity that existed between the two men.

"Joe was at a downtown bar," Steele recalls. "He was celebrating his birthday with forty or so other people, back in the days before Bar Watch. We swept through the gathering and used the *Liquor Control Act* as our reason for doing so.

"Joe was wearing a white golf shirt with a Death Head logo on one side and 'NOMADS' sewn in red lettering on the collar on the other side. One of the officers asked Joe if the inscription said 'Gonads,' which of course riled Joe no end. Joe was with some now-deceased bad dudes. As a police officer, you try to pretend that you're not scared or intimidated, so you walk about with all the confidence and bravado you can muster. They strut as well, a little bit of peacocking going on on both sides."

As Steele remembers it, their conversation went this way:

"Joe, I am going to need to see some ID."

"I don't have any ID with me."

"Well, you can't be in a bar without any ID."

"Come on. You know me."

"Yup, but unfortunately I can't remember when your birthday is. And the law requires you to have not one piece of ID but two, just so that I know you are who you say you are and you're old enough to be in a licensed premises of this type. You're going to have to go and get some ID, Joe, and return with it if you want to stay here."

"But this is my birthday. Come on, man. Everybody is here for me."

"No problem. You can take them all with you. Make it into a house party. No ID required there."

At that point, Steele recalls, Joe lost it. "I told him that if he continued to go down that road I would arrest him for causing a disturbance. 'Is that what you want?' I asked him. 'To spend your birthday in jail?'"

Furious, Joe exited the bar with two women—one on each arm—and summoned a cab. Steele and his partner jumped into their nearby police cruiser, raced up behind the cab and pulled it over. They approached the cab on the driver's side and looked past the driver to Joe sitting in the front passenger seat.

"Joe looks at us and says in a loud voice, rife with frustration, 'What is it now? What? What? What do you want, Brandon?'"

"'Joe,' I say, 'this doesn't concern you.'"

Turning to the cab driver, Steele declared, "You are not licensed to pick up fares in the City of Vancouver. You know that as well as I do. Joe, you're going to have to get out of the cab. Now."

By this time, according to Steele, Joe was beside himself and started berating the cab driver. The last Steele and his partner saw of him, Joe was walking with the two women toward their next destination, wherever that might have been.

In their recollections, Joe and Brandon are in total agreement on one point: the two men did not like each other. Hated each other, as Joe admits, might be closer to the truth.

To Brandon's way of thinking, Joe and his biker brothers were running the city and ruining it. As a police officer, he saw it as his duty to do everything within his power to put a stop to this disturbing trend.

Joe, on the other hand, had set important personal goals: to become a full-patch Nomad and to keep his commitments to himself and his friend Naz. Guys like Brandon Steele were more than an annoyance. They were the enemy. Not only did they get in the way of his career aspirations, they helped put guys like Joe behind bars. On top of that, they often did so with a look that was smug and taunting—a look that clearly got under Joe's skin, just as it was designed to do.

8

PRINCE of Wales Secondary School is a mere twelve kilometres from Templeton Secondary. It might as well be twelve hundred kilometres. While Templeton is solidly working class, PW—as Prince of Wales Secondary is affectionately known to the immediate community—is middle to upper class. Its students come not only from pricey condominiums in the Arbutus corridor but also from majestic homes set back on tree-lined streets in one of Vancouver's richest neighbourhoods, Shaughnessy.

Shortly after Joe Calendino had painstakingly made his mark at Templeton, among a host of other east side schools, Dak Molnar was making his own mark at Prince of Wales. Like Joe, Dak was not particularly attracted to the usual modes of success: academic excellence, community service, or artistic endeavours. Although a top-level ski racer, he was drawn instead to the edgy periphery of the school, where success was measured by your ability to operate outside the school's code of conduct. As Dak tells it, "My dad had his hands full raising me at a time when it was not common for a father to do so on his own. His advice was customarily simple and straightforward: 'If you do anything stupid, son, don't get caught.'"

Dak lived this maxim. He may have been in the midst of problem after problem—one prime example being a grad prank in which the school had to delay opening because of the gallons of motor oil liberally spread around the hallways—but school authorities could never pin anything on Dak. He had mastered the art of keeping his ears open and his mouth closed. Nor could they tie him to any of the underage drinking or pot smoking that happened after hours on the school grounds or in nearby alleys. His yearbook entry upon graduation was a kind of homage to his high school years: "Thanx to MOM & DAD: I owe you one, John Molson and Maryjane."

Although Dak was an accomplished scholar compared with Joe, he never came close to realizing his potential, largely because of his proclivity for skipping classes. His ambitions lay elsewhere, and Dak, like Joe, had a group of friends who looked up to him and stuck with him through times good and bad. Years later, friends from those days still speak with respect about him.

THEY CAME FROM different parts of the city and were several years apart in age. So, how did the lives of Joe Calendino and Dak Molnar end up intersecting? Turn the calendar forward to 2001. Dak was by then working as a realtor in a business that is a central part of his DNA; his father, developer Andre Molnar, has been an iconic figure for years in Vancouver, first in the burgeoning condominium market and later in the commercial real estate sector. Dak took to the business with gusto. When the opportunity arose within the company to broker the purchase of the Hotel Georgia, one of Vancouver's oldest and pre-eminent downtown landmarks, Dak was in. He was especially interested when offered the lease for the nightclub that came with the hotel, initially known as George the Fifth and then, briefly, as the Chameleon Urban Lounge. Dak and his cronies decided to name the club they had assumed control of the Element Sound Lounge.

Dak assembled a rather curious team to run the club. His associates, who included Sam Wainwright, an erstwhile bartender and elementary school friend, and Noel Steen, Dak's closest friend from his PW days, were long on enthusiasm but short on experience in the nightclub field.

"We had no idea what we were doing," Dak recalls. "None of us had run a business before. Only one of the three of us had worked in a bar; the other two had not. But we were popular guys, and within moments of the club opening, it was a huge success. We were using my dough, and Noel's marketing and artsy experience. Sam ran the bar. He was a skilled mixologist—though we didn't call him that in those days—which is why he never had trouble landing work. Wherever he went, many of his west side friends would gather, hoping for free drinks. Occasionally, very occasionally, they got lucky. The interesting thing about Sam, though, was that he was quite a frugal guy. The minute he had his own bar, guess what? No more free drinks."

For a deposit equal to the club's first and last month's rent, plus approximately $200,000 in renovations, financed by a silent investor well known in the entertainment community, Dak, Noel and Sam had the keys to a nightclub. And to the life those keys opened up for them.

At the time Element was getting off the ground and celebrities throughout the city were discovering it, Joe Calendino was a dedicated and earnest H.A. prospect, a hang-around doing his level best to get off the ground in the biker world. His quest to earn the Nomads patch meant spending almost every waking moment with Donny Roming, his sponsor and mentor, and other club members. That eventually led him to the Element Sound Lounge.

As Dak recounts, after the nightclub was up and running, an old friend called him up. When Dak asked his friend what he'd been up to, the friend replied, "I'm running for the Hells Angels." "For real?" Dak asked him.

"Yeah, for real. I've already passed the first level and have the jacket. I'm only two steps away from being a full member." The friend paused. "I hear you have a nightclub now, Dak. Well, guess what? We're coming down this Friday night to see it."

Dak shook his head, placed his hand over the phone and muttered to himself, "Hells Angels—just what I need!" For good reason, he didn't say that aloud to his friend.

As promised, Dak's boyhood friend showed up that Friday night with several members of the club, full-patch guys and others like himself who were striving to reach that pinnacle.

"What struck me at the time," Dak says, "was their kindness. They were real gentlemen. They always took the VIP room. After that first visit, they came every Friday night, until the day the doors closed on the club. And shortly after their first visit, the group included Joe Calendino."

Joe and Dak began to build a friendly relationship at Element, but what really cemented their bond was their shared interest in a strip club three blocks from the Hotel Georgia. Brandi's is one of Vancouver's few remaining "exotic show lounges," arguably the classiest of this dwindling breed. In addition to hosting scores of locals—everyone from stockbrokers celebrating a strong market close to tradesmen coming in after shifts in the downtown building explosion—Brandi's has seen its fair share of celebrities, including Christian Slater, Tara Reid and, most notably, Ben Affleck. Affleck was engaged to singer/actor Jennifer Lopez at the time of his highly publicized visit to the club. When word reached Lopez that her fiancé had been more than a little active at Brandi's and later with strippers at a party, Lopez called their engagement off.

"Joe would frequently be at Brandi's with a couple of other hang-arounds," Dak recalls. "With Joe, there were always several ladies around. That is really where our relationship formed, chilling with the ladies on the couch. But at the time, it was a fairly loose and informal social thing."

Dak and Joe's connection deepened when they discovered another common interest: Brandon Steele of the Vancouver Police Department. Dak had also incurred Constable Steele's scrutiny. "Brandon hated the fact there were bikers hanging out in my nightclub," Dak says. "He made a serious point of letting me know this. What was clear at the time, to me and everyone else who worked at the club, was that Brandon had a special contempt for Joe Calendino."

Life in Vancouver nightclubs in the early 2000s was a bit of a free-for-all. That changed with the introduction by the VPD of a program called Bar Watch, which was designed to curtail the comings and goings of known gang members at bars, nightclubs and restaurants in the city. Bar Watch was strictly voluntary. The establishments that joined would report to the VPD any guests who were known gangsters, a fact not lost on the Hells Angels. The VPD would then show up at the establishment and remove the men. Soon, the pressure was on for Dak to join the program.

"The VPD came down and said they wanted me to join Bar Watch. I said no. They told me that every time an organized criminal came into your bar, you had to rat them out and get the police to come down there," Dak says. "The rules have changed now. But back then, I had to personally make the call and 'drop the dime' on them. Now, these guys had never picked a fight in my club; they tipped the waitresses as much or more than other customers; and they stuck to their little section and felt good about being able to go somewhere without hassle. I said to Brandon, 'Do you go to Safeway and tell the owner, when a biker wants to buy groceries, you should not sell him groceries?' He told me the two situations were not the same.

"'Yes it is,' I said. 'I have a licence to sell retail alcohol just like the guy at Safeway has a business licence to sell groceries. My job is not to sell to anyone who is intoxicated or to a minor— full stop.'"

Dak concedes that as Vancouver has evolved, the Bar Watch program has been a good thing for the city. At the time, though, he felt otherwise. The result was a deep divide between him and the VPD—and an increasingly close relationship between him and Joe.

ELEMENT MAY NOT have seen the first-hand results of what could happen when gang members frequent night-clubs—though a shooting took place outside its doors in June 2003—but other clubs were not so lucky. There was the shoot-ing of Donny Roming at Bar None. Even more chilling was the August 2003 shooting at Loft Six, another Vancouver club, where an argument broke out between two groups of men. In another strange coincidence, Roming was the club's former owner. Loft Six, like Dak's Element Sound Lounge, was not on the Bar Watch registry.

One newspaper report about the worst nightclub shooting in the city's history read:

> When bullets started flying at the Loft Six nightclub in Gas-town Saturday morning, panicked patrons "began crawling over top of each other" in an effort to get out of the way, a bystander said Monday.
>
> The fusillade killed two men—one of them an uninvolved bystander—and a third man also died in circumstances police believe may be related to the shootings at Loft Six. Seven others were injured, of whom at least two were also

bystanders, including well-known Los Angeles dance instructor Steven Stanton, who was shot in the back.

That was nearly it for Joe, who had happened to be in Loft Six when the bullets started flying. He escaped unscathed. The shootings changed things for Dak. He realized that Vancouver had become a different city and that being a nightclub owner, Bar Watch member or not, put him and his staff squarely in the crosshairs.

"After the shooting outside Element—two weeks before the Loft Six debacle—we had had enough. We agreed with the owner of the hotel to close the doors," he says. "My real estate career was moving in the right direction. Noel had figured out another business. Sam moved along and ran many bars after that. We decided the risk-reward equation was too heavily weighted to the risk side. We had got everything we wanted out of the experience. We met girls. We hung out with celebrities. We got to know and hang out with some of the city's renegades. It was rather romantic at the time, but there is no romance in it for me anymore. It's ugly. Plain ugly. It's a bloodbath. I didn't always believe what I read in those days. I thought things could not be as bad as was being reported. In hindsight, I realize they were."

Nonetheless, Dak looks back on those days with a kind of wistfulness. "There's an old saying that if you're going to have crime—which every country does—it's better to have organized crime than unorganized crime. Back in the day, if there was a fight, it was usually with fists. Then, all of a sudden, these guys had all watched *Scarface* or something, and they began using guns. With that came the power struggle. When the drug-trade pie began to get chopped up into smaller and smaller pieces—and this is true of any capitalist market, as witnessed in the auto industry—you get more competition. The next thing you know, there were all these upstart gangs. They seemed to be springing up everywhere, all getting armed to the teeth and fighting over the same shrinking pieces of the pie. Suddenly, guys were killing each other over nothing. What we have left now is a bunch of teenagers with a half pound of coke in one pocket and a gun in the other."

Joe, recalls Dak, had passion in his eyes during the time of their three-year friendship. But Joe's substance abuse was well underway by then and getting worse. His behaviour was increasingly self-destructive, Dak noticed. He and Joe maintained their friendship for six months or so after Element closed. After that, Joe disappeared into the lifestyle he had worked so feverishly to attain.

9

JOE became a full-patch member of the Nomads, the charter he had pursued with relentless determination. During those years, as a "one percenter"—a term coined by outlaw motorcyclists who viewed themselves as living outside the boundaries favoured by 99 percent of civilized society—Joe lived high off the hog. He married Linda, a young woman from north Burnaby, and a short time later they were blessed with a son named Guiseppe, born in 2002. Their son Luca was born five years later. Papa, as Joe liked to be called, loved his sons with all his heart, just as his dad loved Joe and his siblings.

But Joe was never certain he would get through the day in one piece. When he said goodbye to Jo Jo, as he called his firstborn, Joe made sure of two things. One, he checked that the Glock he carried with him at all times was tucked securely into his belt, out of reach of tiny hands. Two, he never gave his son a kiss or hug in the exposed doorway of their home. Without exception, the two of them said their goodbyes behind the protective shelter of an exterior wall.

Each morning when I said goodbye I would make sure that my son was not visible to the street. He would put his little arms around me and say, "Papa, I love you." I would look at him and just want to make sure that I saw him again that night. "I love you too, son," I would respond. But I always wondered, "Is this the last time I will say these words?"

———

Joe's siblings, Ralph and Eva, were also parents by this time, and they began to fear for their own children. They did not want Joe coming around, in case he was the target of people who wanted him out of the picture. Just as Joe's number-one priority was the safety of his family, his brother and sister were protective of their own children: Eva's daughter, Caterina, and Ralph's children, Sal and Annissa, both in high school. Sharing Joe's last name, the two Calendinos were particularly vulnerable, mistaken identity being not uncommon in the world of gang hits.

"We loved our brother," says Eva today. "But we sure as hell did not want him placing our kids at risk."

Joe was also a frequent target of police surveillance teams. In their presentation at Vancouver schools, as well as in the broader community, VPD officers Doug Spencer and Adam Dhaliwal showed slides of some of the most notorious gangsters in Vancouver's Lower Mainland. Joe was among them. So were others who had not been so lucky, people like Jimmy Van Sang Nguyen, whose bullet-riddled body was shown lying lifeless in front of a stylish yellow sports car. There was also Tuan Van Le, shown with blood running down his body after being slaughtered in a gang-related feud. He was fifteen years old.

Joe was frequently found in cars stopped by the police. Usually not driving and not carrying any identification, he would answer the question "Your name, please?" with a cocky "Johnny Seatbelts." The Vancouver Police Department listed that in its database entry as his alias. Joe was confident, no doubt about it, and he seemed to be invincible.

From the outside, Joe's life looked glamorous. At first, he travelled widely: California, Las Vegas, Rio de Janeiro, Montreal and New York. In Italy he had a chance to connect with various members of the extended Calendino family. Photos from those days depict a smiling Joe alongside other members of the club, with iconic tourist attractions serving as backdrops: Rio's Christ the Redeemer and Italy's Tower of Pisa among them.

However, his jet-setting ways came to an abrupt halt after September 11, 2001. "All of a sudden," Joe recalls, "there was a complete shutdown at the borders when guys tried to go into various parts of Europe, except perhaps Italy. It maintained a fairly open-door policy, unlike France, where I had travelled to earlier but could not enter following 9/11."

During these years, Joe was constantly in trouble with the law. The following charges and convictions represent only the most egregious publicly recorded examples:

2003: Convicted of carrying a loaded and restricted weapon, a .45 calibre semi-automatic handgun, which fell from his waistband during a police interrogation outside a nightclub.

2007: Convicted of assault in a barroom fight that took place at the Lake City Casino in Kelowna, British Columbia, in 2005. At the time, Joe was wearing his H.A. colours, and he was captured on the casino's surveillance video. The story gained prominence when clips were shown on various newscasts throughout the province and nationally.

2008: Charged with trafficking in a controlled substance. In 2010, Joe pleaded guilty to the charge.

What this list of convictions doesn't tell us is what Joe's day-to-day life looked like. On one not atypical evening, he saved the life of a friend by the narrowest of margins.

———

The night started off like any Saturday night. I'm having dinner at a very nice restaurant with a girlfriend named Connie, who later became the mother of two kids outside my marriage, Matteo and Dominic. The phone's persistent ringing interrupts our conversation. I answer it. On the other end, I hear the frantic voice of one of my good friends, who owes me a sum of money, a fairly large sum. He is crying, hysterical. Someone, he says, is going to kill him. Not trying to kill him. Not threatening to kill him. Going to kill him.

I'm not impressed that he owes me and others money, but I know that I'm going to end up helping out this guy anyway. That's who I am, how I'm hard-wired. He tells me that some people—probably those that are about to kill him, I'm guessing—want to see me. Me? I don't get it. It's not up to me to listen to what they want. It's up to my friend. I agree to see them, though, hearing the urgency in this guy's voice, knowing my response could mean the difference between him living or landing at the bottom of the Fraser River to become fish fodder.

I get off the phone and tell Connie that I have to excuse myself, that I have some business that must be attended to. I make arrangements to get some of my guys together to deal with this matter.

We arrive at the agreed-upon meeting place, our strategic plan of cars and "toys" squarely in place. They show up equally well-prepared, which means equally well-armed.

As soon as "their guy"—I'll call him Liam—walks in, I realize I know him. We sit down, the tension in the room somewhere between the stratosphere and the blackness of space. The meeting starts. I can tell right away that they are trying to show their presence (i.e., intimidate us), just as we are trying to intimidate them; they want to let us know they mean business.

I lay down the law right away: "If he dies [the guy who made the frantic call], then you owe me the money he owes me."

"Hold on, what about our money?" Liam counters, clearly pissed.

"Not my issue. I want him released, and I want him released now."

Eventually, and rather reluctantly, they agree to let my friend go. What I discovered later was that they had beaten him badly, very badly. They cracked his skull with a baseball bat, chopped his Achilles tendon with a small machete and beat him with the bat elsewhere. Somehow—I don't know how—he survived. He was lucky. Most of these situations do not turn out this way.

This "friend" still owes me the money, a not-insubstantial sum. So if you think there is some kind of honour between brothers, think again. I'll never see a dime of it. Trust no one. Trust lives within your family. Period. My dad was right.

There was another time Joe faced a dilemma not uncommon to the world of drugs and debt he inhabited.

I was told I had a decision to make. A friend of mine owed money to others, a large sum of money, about $300,000. The order that I received was simple: either shoot up his parents' place so that he knew we meant business or find some other, equally effective way to scare him into settling this debt.

I let my own moral code get in the way. "What do his parents have to do with this?" I pondered. I decided not to go after them. Instead, I personally paid the debt of $300K. Some question my decision. Sometimes I wonder myself if I was a fucking idiot for doing this. But in my heart I know I did the right thing. Either way, I was going to lose. Shoot up the parents' home, and now it's a fight to the death with him. On the other hand, he might be so desperate that he turns me in to the cops and I go to jail.

As well, he would likely have ended up doing the same thing to my house by way of retaliation—or even to my parents' house. My two children and my wife would be sitting ducks. If that happened or if he went after my parents, the result would be death. No ifs, ands or buts about it. I would have killed him if he didn't get me first.

With drugs, it's always complicated. It's rarely just about the money. There's always something else at play. Interestingly, most of these guys are now dead.

––––––––

Drugs were complicating Joe's own life as well. Because of his increasingly out-of-control substance abuse, his trajectory within the club was already on the downswing. The brawl in Kelowna was seen by most television viewers as an example of a biker laying a beating on a guy who had knocked over the biker's gambling chips. If you don't want trouble with a Hells Angel, the moral seemed to be, don't mess with him—or his chips. Those who knew Joe saw something else in this TV piece. Drugs were playing a greater and greater role in Joe's life, consuming more and more of his energy, his health and his time. He had moved from socially acceptable drugs—alcohol and marijuana—to much harder stuff. With that transition came the potential for much graver consequences.

––––––––

The feeling you get from GHB [gamma-hydroxybutyrate] and crack cocaine is unlike anything you have ever felt. It makes you go to places that you cannot explain. I decided to hide my addiction from everyone because it gave me a place to hide my grief, my sadness. I was in the process of losing everything and I knew it.

––––––––

But while Joe thought he was hiding his habit from those around him, three people knew better, his mother among them.

––––––––

It's funny. People say your mom knows everything. It's true. You see, my mother and I are really close. She was the only person

who asked me if there were any other drugs I was involved with.
I was shocked. I was in complete denial.

———

Joe's siblings, Ralph and Eva, were onto him as well. They had
sensed for years that Joe's drug use was getting worse, even if
they had no evidence to back up their suspicions.

Eva recalls picking up Joe from jail after the 2003 handgun
charge. "I told him, 'Joe, you stink. You cry about your time
here. You've been here for all of one week. You put us through
hell for weeks on end. You keep going the way you're going, and
you're going to end up in there for life. Or dead. Think about it.
In jail for life—or dead. Take your pick. Either way you die.' I
was always the one who was never afraid to say anything to him.
Mom and Dad, he was their oldest. He was their shining star. If
anyone was going to do great, it was Joe."

Frank in particular was at a loss as to what to do. He lived
with a tremendous sense of guilt, something he confided to
Eva. "If I could have done things differently," he lamented, "but
I didn't know better."

Increasingly, Joe's behaviour was also coming under scrutiny within the Hells Angels. He was less predictable than he
had been, more obviously addicted to drugs. At some point,
they worried, he might bring the club the type of attention
they worked hard to avoid. The Kelowna incident was the final
straw, and Joe was forced to turn in his patch shortly thereaf-
ter. Rather than serving as a wake-up call, though, this period
in Joe's life seemed to spawn an even greater dependency on
drugs. GHB and crack replaced his "brothers" as his best
friends.

———

People say once you start smoking crack, you are done for.
There is no turning back. I know what they are talking about.

I was chatting on the phone one evening with one of my
friends from high school. I put down the phone when my oldest

son walked into the room at about ten thirty. He wanted to go and play soccer in the backyard. Crazy, I know.

Now, most reasonable parents would simply say, "Time for bed, Jo Jo. It's already ten thirty!" Not me. I was still high from a full day of doing drugs. You see, my love and passion for my children made my drug-induced high elevate to a whole new level; it made it even better. I quickly accepted my son's invitation and headed for the backyard.

They say that sex is the peak of the mountain when you're high, but I have discovered there is no sex that can replace the love I have for my children. There is no sex that feels as good as your child saying, "Papa, I love you."

Hugs and kisses. My boys are my world, even though the last two years of my drug addiction made that world a living hell.

––––––––

Both Joe's marriage and the other significant relationship that he had were now on the rocks, the result of two factors. The first was Joe's dependence on drugs. The second was what he calls his "lack of honesty" with women. At that point in his life, he was not capable of fidelity or honesty with anyone, traits that tend to go hand in hand. Looking back, he has nothing but respect for his two exes, Linda and Connie.

––––––––

Both Linda and Connie have been to hell and back with me and still remain among the most dedicated mothers I have ever seen. No woman should have to put up with all the crap they had to deal with. I cannot blame either of them for a single thing. Whatever happened, and whatever has happened since, I own.

God blessed me with four wonderful children, far beyond anything a man can reasonably expect or, in my case, deserve.

––––––––

Joe appeared to be hitting bottom, as alcohol and drug counsellors are wont to say. But in this case, appearance and reality were not the same thing. He still had a long way down to go—a near-fatal distance at that.

Even the Vancouver Police Department was aware that Joe, a gangster once respected in the world of organized crime, was in a serious freefall. As VPD sergeant Kevin Torvik says, "Joe was seen in the skids of Vancouver and Surrey. He was 'cracked out' all the time."

The story of Joe's descent into the world of addiction is filled with both pathos and irony. Through it we see the potential in each of us to become enslaved to something so powerful that friends and family no longer carry meaning. In that world, the next drink or the next fix is always more important than your child's Little League ball game or a walk along the shoreline with your loved one. Dishonesty and duplicity become your constant companions.

One irony is that, for years, Joe had harangued his sister, Eva, to go easy on alcohol. He was a kind of temperance priest in that respect.

"I was angry," Eva recalls. "Here was this guy who was against drugs and alcohol, at least with me. He certainly was not a heavy drinker at the time. We would go to a club and Joe would say, 'What are you drinking? What's wrong with Perrier water?' And he would make this big scene so that I, his kid sister, switched to something non-alcoholic. Kind of crazy, isn't it, when you look back."

By this time, Joe was back living in his parents' home. But he would be gone for days at a time, increasingly drawn into a dark world that few of us ever see. Rat-infested crack houses. Heroin junkies who would rob you blind to obtain their next fix. Discarded, often contaminated, needles strewn about on garbage-littered floors. Joe, a formerly proud man, was reduced to combing back alleys for anything that might help him get his next fix.

A young Frank Calendino (holding dog's paw) with Nerina's brother, Frank Carnivale.

Frank and Nerina take a calming break during their wedding reception.

Joe, Ralph and Eva shortly before their near-fatal car trip with their mom through the Fraser Canyon.

Fit and ready—
Joe's foray into
kickboxing.

"Little Rocky" was Joe's aptly earned nickname. Here he wears the autographed
gloves and shorts from Stallone's *Rocky IV*.

A happy occasion:
long-time friend
Andy Amoroso's
wedding night.

Joe as part of the wedding party for Paolo Fusco, sister Eva's brother-in-law.

Joe, third from left, with his high school buddies enjoying time in Hawaii.

Training with a fellow combatant prior to bouts in Tacoma, Washington.

Joe, in his early twenties, sports the gold medal he earned at the Tiger Balm International tourney.

Pushing himself to his physical limits.

Employing mind over matter, Joe breaks a baseball bat with his bare shin.

Fishing in Mexico: Joe on the right, Rob Cortese on the left.

Joe's state-of-the-art Vancouver store design.

Joe enjoying the high-end car stereo system he has just installed in a new Porsche.

With Nez, the indomitable general manager of Joe's cell phone operations.

Coaching a youth soccer team, a sport Joe loves to this day.

At a beach near
Rome with
cousin Leonora.

Joe with Nona Eva at his wedding in 2000.

A proud new dad
holding son Jo Jo.

Proud parents Nerina
and Frank pose for
this photo at daughter
Eva's wedding.

Joe's first Harley, the beginning of his ride into the world of motorcycle clubs.

Joe with two of his closest companions from this era.

Joe and unidentified prospect proudly sport their bottom rockers on the day they received them.

Joe's first day wearing the full patch—a day of wild celebration with hundreds of partiers.

Joe outside
Osaka's, one of
his favourite
restaurant haunts.

Joe joins others
in celebrating
the twentieth
anniversary of a
H.A. chapter.

Master Chen teaches Joe Chinese qigong, used by martial artists to increase power and energy.

Joe's arrest photo following his altercation with Brandon Steele in downtown Vancouver.

Joe's mugshot following his arrest for trafficking in cocaine in Surrey, BC.

The advertising poster from *Let Me Up*, the critically acclaimed play inspired by Joe's life and performed at Templeton Secondary School.

The first Yo Bro logo.

YBYG youth excel in a martial arts tournament.

YBYG's updated logo reflects the inclusion of girls as an essential part of its mission.

There is no way to explain this world, this hell—staying in a place that is infested with rats, infested with crack and heroin junkies. The amount of money that went through one of those places in the normal course of a day made it look more like a prosperous day-trading company than a dilapidated crack house. It was staggering, crazy.

———

At first, even Joe's family had little understanding of the depth to which he had fallen. Sure, Ralph and Eva knew Joe's life had taken a serious turn for the worse when he began drinking heavily. This was not the brother they had known. But Joe tried to hide the worst of it: the blood that flowed from his nose because of excessive cocaine use, the dirt that was permanently caked under his fingernails from scrounging back alleys, the desperation in his ebony-dark eyes as he tried to scrape together enough money for more drugs.

Frank and Nerina were deeply concerned, but like many parents in this situation, they simply did not know what to do. "Terrified" might be an apt description of how they felt. Joe had changed. He had entered a world they had no knowledge of, a world inhabited by people who were as strange to them as aliens. When Joe had been a respected member of the Nomads, they'd felt they knew what he was up to—at least to some extent. This new world, this new Joe, left them reeling. Once robust and healthy, Joe now looked dreadful, pathetic. He was gaunt, and the colour had drained from his face. Putting pride aside, the family members turned to each other for help.

The Calendino family was the true brotherhood. Whatever Joe's current problems were, his parents and his siblings would be there for him—as difficult as that might be. As Frank was fond of saying, "Friends are friends. They come and go in your life. But family is there forever—they have your back from the time you are born until the time you die." That was the philosophy the Calendinos lived by, through good times and bad. And these days for Joe were definitely of the bad variety.

———

You somehow got in and wanted to be part of this world [drug use and addiction]. The people—well, let's just say they were demons. But we were all on this pathway together. Your entry into it was subtle, almost hypnotic. You slid deeper and deeper into this lifestyle without even knowing that it was happening. At some point you found yourself at the bottom of a chasm with no apparent way out. You were the one, the only one, who made the decision to go there. You were the only one with the power, ultimately, to figure out how to get yourself out.

———

While Joe's siblings and parents continued to love and support him as best they could, the extended Calendino clan had serious qualms and a certain degree of embarrassment, which divided the family. Particularly affected by Joe's lifestyle was his uncle Pietro, Frank's younger brother. While Pietro was careful not to criticize Joe publicly, privately he knew that his own good name had been tarnished by their association—never a good thing in the turbulent and often savage world of politics.

Eva's response, representative of her side of the family, was blunt. "Tough, Uncle Peter. When it comes to gangsters and politicians, what's the fucking difference? I'd rather have a gangster running the city telling you exactly where your money is going than a politician who says thank-you while stuffing it into his own pocket."

Joe was more than merely lost by this point in his life. He was angry, and he did not know where to focus his rage. He no longer felt safe in his own neighbourhood, but he was unsure how to change that. It wasn't that he feared for himself. He feared for his family. He had rolled his entire holdings on a high-stakes lifestyle and ended up losing it all. His life had come up craps.

Small wonder, therefore, that for him alcohol and drugs had a magnetic, even therapeutic quality to them.

At some point, Joe left the comfort of his parents' home for the street. He would occasionally show up at the family home unannounced, engaging in conversation with his folks and whoever else happened to be there. He would eat heartily, enjoying Nerina's home-cooked meals. The food stimulated memories that took him back to his boyhood. Playing in the hills of Kamloops with his cousin Tony. Working new rhythmic patterns on his drum kit in East Vancouver. Savouring the first splash of ice water after a game of soccer played hard but fair. Inevitably, though, these images would be supplanted by more forceful ones, urges that started somewhere deep within him and soon took shape as a compulsion. Time for another "fix." When that happened, Joe would jump up, say goodbye and be on his way. Where to, the family was never quite sure.

SURREY IS ONE of Canada's fastest-growing and largest cities. With a population soon expected to eclipse that of Vancouver, its better-known neighbour to the west, Surrey has experienced the trials and tribulations common to rapidly expanding communities. Foremost among these has been criminal activity associated with the drug trade. The city has been lauded for its recent efforts to address the problem and praised for its forward-thinking council. At the time Joe was frequenting the city, though, Surrey was where many of the Lower Mainland's addicts headed.

A lack of familiarity with Surrey's byways and alleyways did not stop Joe's siblings from trying to help him. Both Ralph and Eva found themselves on various occasions attempting to track Joe down. Their efforts started initially in the back alleys of Vancouver's West End. If no Joe was to be found there, they shifted their focus to East Van. Following that, they fanned farther afield to Surrey.

Eva would rouse herself out of bed at two or three in the morning—the hour didn't matter. She was worried about Joe, and she would tell her husband, Nick, what she had to do. Caterina, their daughter, sleeping soundly through the night down the hall, would be greeted in the morning by a mom who was unusually tired as she prepared the family for work and school, then set off for her own job at the laundry, which started at 7 a.m. Ralph's wife, Rina, also paid a price, worried as she was for the safety of her husband and children.

Most often, Eva and Ralph didn't find Joe. But once in a while they hit the jackpot. There was one early morning when Eva jumped into her van and headed east on Highway 1. Her sources—mutual friends and members of the extended family— had told her that Joe had been sighted near the SkyTrain station on King George Highway in Surrey. Eva was familiar with the area, having been there before. Usually, by the time she got somewhere, Joe was nowhere to be found. But she sensed this time would be different. If Joe was anywhere within view or earshot, she was determined to catch up with him, even if it meant parking the van and chasing him on foot.

Her sisterly intuition proved correct. She spotted Joe amid a group of addicts huddled together at the foot of the escalator leading to the SkyTrain platform. As Eva pulled alongside, she and Joe made eye contact. Within nano-seconds, he had bolted from the group and hightailed it up the escalator.

Eva swung her van right up over the curb, and in one fluid motion she was out and running. She did not even bother to turn off the engine. The few bedraggled junkies who looked on might have thought they were watching a real-life episode of *Rookie Blue*. Instead, they were viewing the desperation of a sister who loved her brother and was doing everything within her power to get him back.

Joe got away that time. He usually did. Despite his increasing drug use and the diminution of his once-powerful body, he was still remarkably agile and fit. Eva returned to her van dispirited and angry. She was saddened by the sorry state into which her brother had descended and furious that once again she had been torn from the comfort of her bed in a fruitless effort to help him. Amazingly, no one had touched Eva's vehicle, despite the fact that with its motor still running, it was a gift just waiting to be unwrapped by thieves. She smiled grimly at the absurdity of it all.

Another time, Eva was cruising with singular intensity near the BC Lions' practice facility in Surrey. She spotted what looked like a group of addicts huddled in a nearby alleyway. As she turned slowly toward the group, high beams illuminating their gaunt, unshaven faces, she spotted Joe. The moment he realized it was Eva, he was off like Ben Johnson on steroids.

Eva knew she could not catch him on foot. She jammed on the brakes, put the van in park and dashed over to one of Joe's alleyway "friends." "You," she said to him. "Take this ten bucks. Go and get that guy, and bring him back to me."

The startled man set off in the direction in which they'd seen Joe vanish. Neither Joe nor his suddenly richer-by-ten-dollars sidekick appeared again that night.

The lowest points of all for Eva were the crack houses. She had become so desperate she no longer feared entering them. On more than one occasion she kicked in a door, demanding that the stunned occupants give up her brother.

"You'd be amazed at what comes over you," she says. "Looking back, I can't believe I did what I did. If you asked me to do that today, there is no way I could. At the time, though, I was on a mission. I wanted to find Joe. I wanted to know he was alive. I wanted to know he was warm. I wanted to know he was fed and safe."

The effect on Eva's marriage was predictable. Her husband, Nick, was bitter about Joe's addiction coming between him and the woman he loved. Eva remained resolute.

"Imagine it was one of *your* brothers or sisters," she beseeched her husband one evening. "You would want to do the same for any of them, and I would understand, totally. I would understand because that's how love, deep love, works. Don't ask me to make a decision between you and my brother. We don't want to go there." It was the last time the topic came up for discussion between them.

Despite eluding Eva when she came looking for him, Joe often reached out to her when he needed money. Be it ten dollars or twenty, Joe would inform her that he was in a tight spot and needed her help. Eva would boil inside, knowing that whatever she "loaned" Joe would go straight into his body in the form of crack or to a dealer to whom he owed money. But try as she might to say no, she couldn't. She knew she would not be able to live with herself if she turned down Joe's request and he ended up dead.

On one occasion when Joe appeared at the Calendino home for Sunday dinner, his hands were black and his feet raw from walking aimlessly through the streets of the Lower Mainland. His rancid body odour reminded the family that he had not had a shower in several days, maybe longer. They were shocked, but they reminded themselves that he was still alive. And as long as he was alive, there was hope.

10

THE first thing you notice about Sergeant Kevin
Torvik of the Vancouver Police Department
is that he looks much younger than his forty-
five years. Tall and fit with longish brown hair and brown eyes,
Torvik is, in some respects, the antithesis of Joe Calendino.
Joe has lived life hard, much of it on the wrong side of the law;
Kevin has lived life with equal intensity, but on the right side of
the law. The two men are within twelve months of each other in
age, and they have much in common. Both attended Templeton
Secondary School, Joe graduating in 1985, Kevin a year later.
Both had the utmost respect for Jim Crescenzo, the school's
revered drama teacher. Both possessed leadership qualities
from the time they were kids, and both were influenced by the
communities in which they grew up. Both were drawn to crime
as well, Joe to make it his life, Kevin to do everything in his
power to put a stop to it.

As an eleven-year-old, Torvik found himself in the role of
the man of the house. His father had died suddenly, leaving his
mother to raise the children on her own. Arriving home from

school one afternoon, Torvik discovered that their house had been broken into, the family's possessions scattered everywhere. Years later, the fury in his voice is palpable as he recalls this event. "I was angry. I wanted to get that person who did it—not for myself, but because it hurt Mom. She had worked so hard for absolutely everything we had."

As a teen, Torvik witnessed a fight at Hastings Park. What had started out as a pre-arranged scrap between two girls took an ugly turn when the park attendant tried to intervene. The focus shifted from the two combatants to the attendant himself. Several people in the crowd swarmed him and mercilessly beat him.

"He was only doing his job," Torvik says, "trying to do the right thing. It was so wrong, and yet I felt so helpless. I thought to myself, 'If only I could get in a position where I could help someone like that. If only.'"

Following graduation from Simon Fraser University and five years spent living in Japan, Torvik applied and was accepted into the Vancouver Police Department. He completed his training, and corrective laser surgery to his eyes removed the last obstacle facing him in his quest to become a police officer. Torvik requested placement in Vancouver's District 2, a vast area that includes the neighbourhood where he and Joe had grown up.

"It made the placement a lot easier, growing up in the East End," he says. "You saw many shades of grey, because you had not lived a sheltered existence. There were very few instances of straight black and white."

From District 2 patrol, Torvik soon transitioned into the drug squad. He spent time undercover and then joined a small unit known within the VPD as the OMGU, the Outlaw Motorcycle Gang Unit. After this, it did not take long for his life and Joe's to intersect.

The OMGU was designed to make trouble for us, plain and simple. That was the sole reason for their existence. We hated their fucking guts—every single person connected to them.

———

Like most students at Templeton, Torvik had viewed Joe as one of the toughest guys around. But there was more to Joe than fighting prowess, in Torvik's mind. Joe had other qualities Torvik found compelling, one being leadership, the other a clearly defined sense of justice. "Joe was the kind of guy you would call to beat up the bully," Torvik recalls. But a feel-good reunion between two former schoolmates was not in the cards. Torvik had a job to do. Joe hated cops.

Although they had a passing acquaintance while students at Templeton, the first actual meeting between the two stands out— at least in Torvik's mind. Joe was living in a nicely appointed house near Notre Dame Regional Secondary School, an independent Catholic school on Renfrew Street to the southeast of Templeton. As Joe polished his car in the alley behind his house, Torvik and his partner approached.

"Joe recognized me from our days at Templeton, not that we hung out together or anything like that. I said to him, 'Hey, how's it going? I just want to let you know I'm working for Larry Butler [head of the OMGU].' I think his reaction was something like 'Get the fuck out of here.'"

Nonetheless, the seed for a future relationship had been sown. "A while later, there was the incident in Kelowna where a couple of members of the H.A. got into a fight with others in a bar," Torvik says. "One of those members turned out to be Joe. But he wasn't arrested there, contrary to popular belief. He was arrested outside his house in Vancouver. We ended up taking him back to Kelowna, and that was the starting point for the media circus that ensued. That was also the beginning of the end as far as Joe's involvement with the H.A. was concerned."

Like others, Torvik was aware that Joe's drug use was spiralling out of control. On at least two occasions, he got calls from colleagues in patrol who let him know that Joe had overdosed and was at St. Paul's Hospital in downtown Vancouver.

"Every cop in Vancouver knew Joe," Torvik says. "Many knew that I knew Joe personally as well, and so they would call me. I went to see Joe and told him, 'You know what, buddy, it's only going to get worse. You are living a death sentence. You better figure that out before death comes knocking.'"

Joe didn't want to hear it. Maybe Kevin's words were too close to the truth. Or maybe he just didn't care anymore. His love of being high seemed to trump anything else left in his pathetically shattered life.

The call that Kevin received in April 2008 was different. It came from a colleague in the Surrey detachment of the RCMP.

"We have Joe in jail," the caller told Torvik.

"For what?" Torvik asked.

"For trying to sell a $10 rock to an undercover officer."

Torvik made a quick decision. Once again, he would visit Joe to see what he might be able to do to help. On the drive to Surrey, he reflected on the terrible irony that was now Joe's life. Here was a guy who had once been a millionaire gangster and was now incarcerated for trying to sell a $10 chunk of crack cocaine. How the mighty are fallen, thought Kevin. Many people in Torvik's position would have felt that Joe was getting his just deserts. But Torvik refused to lose sight of the man enmeshed in this tragedy.

"On the way out, I picked up some food for Joe," he says. "I picked up a bag of McDonald's. Some burgers, some fries. That kind of stuff. When I got there, Joe was lying in his cell in the fetal position. His hair was dishevelled. He weighed about 110 pounds, certainly not much more. A shadow of the man I had known. In short, he was a mess. Joe tugged the bag of food from my hand, and the contents were gone in minutes. He was like a starving dog. Obviously, he had not eaten in days.

"We had a long chat, probably four hours at least. At one point, Joe looked at me and said through tear-rimmed eyes, 'I don't want this to happen to anyone, Kevin. No one. Someday, I want to work with kids so that they don't have to go through this.' 'Are you kidding me?' I asked him. 'In the condition you're in? Unless you work on getting better, you won't be working with anyone, young or old.'"

But if people thought Joe had finally hit bottom with this latest arrest, they were proved wrong once again.

Shortly after his release, Joe was back on a multi-day high, a mixture of cocaine and whatever it was cut with—probably speed—ripping through his system. In a drug-fuelled haze, he and a couple of other guys began arguing over something inconsequential. Crack-house confrontations were like this, triggered by things so microscopic they do not merit remembering. In spite of Joe's debilitated and drug-addled state, he was still a formidable foe. Call it muscle memory or simply violence unleashed: when the situation began to escalate, he was ready to fight to the finish, even to the death if necessary.

Joe came very close to death that evening. One of his assailants was armed with a bat. He swung it at Joe with a force so hard it would have killed most people, connecting just below Joe's skull on the right side. The crack of breaking bone was audible. Joe's jaw shattered, imploding inward. He began toppling, and he was unconscious before he hit the ground.

Despite the intense pain he was experiencing when he came to, Joe somehow picked himself off the concrete and stumbled to the nearest hospital. The pain continued to escalate, barely eased by the painkillers he was given. What they could never ease was the pain his pathetic life had become. "Why me," he asked himself as he lay in his hospital bed. "Why me?"

As he pondered the question, he came to the realization that he had just entered the biggest fight of his life. It wasn't a street brawl, nothing resembling the kind of conflict he was used to. The fight he had embarked on raged within himself and nowhere else—his addiction. Joe knew that if his life was ever to regain purpose, he had to get clean. He started by refusing any further pain medication, choosing to endure pain that would crush most people.

The doctor tried to convince me otherwise, but I told him, "Doc, what you need to realize is that it was drugs that got me here in the first place. Call me crazy if you want, but now that I have hope to get clean for the first time in months, maybe years, I can't go back to any type of drug, legal or not."

Joe's jaw was swollen, bruised and battered. He could barely move it. He was able to speak only with determination, and over the protestations of the doctor who advised him not to. An incision in his neck, directly underneath where the blow had landed, allowed the yellow and blood-red fluid to drain into a thick rectangle of gauze that had to be changed every couple of hours.

Joe may have looked broken. However, he was anything but. As he began his slow recovery, he felt an infusion of hope, something he had not experienced for a long time. He felt that his life was already starting to change in a positive way, taking a turn where sobriety would replace drug dependency. No longer would he need to run from his friends and family out of embarrassment or fear.

To an outsider, Joe appeared to be in terrible shape—a "human train wreck," as someone described him at the time. But those who knew him well saw something they had not seen in Joe in years. There was purpose in his eyes. Some even detected a sense of optimism.

Addicts tell you almost without exception that, while the challenge to attain sobriety is theirs alone, the people who help them play a critical role. For Joe, that support group consisted of his family and some loyal friends who had stood by him.

———

I have a great family and friends. My mom, who I call the "prison guard," watched over me 24/7. My brother, Ralph, was my saviour who said, "I will die before I lose you again." Then there was my sister, Eva, who was the "sergeant-at-arms." There simply is no fear in that girl. Of course, my dad had taught me lessons that can only be learned in the school of love and hard knocks. If there is anyone who would take on the world, it was him. He could put fear into anybody. Like he said on one occasion to one of the most feared individuals in the Vancouver area, "I am clinically insane, and I have done my time, and I will kill you and your family if anything happens to my son." They had all spent many nights crying and wondering whether I was dead or alive. They spent hours and days, weeks and years, looking for me to find my soul again. I am eternally grateful.

———

First and foremost among Joe's loyal friends was Andy Amoroso, rock-steady as always. There was Roberto, another of his high school friends, whom Joe had made a point of avoiding for the past few years. "I didn't want him to see me like that," Joe says. As well, there was Jimmy, "the man with the heart of gold." There was one of Roberto's brothers, Ramano, who realized that if Joe was to begin his journey afresh, he'd need the support of permanent employment and stability in his life. Ramano provided it. There was Victor, the "guy from the car stereo shop," who inspired Joe and stood by him. There was Nez, the one-time general manager of Joe's company, who sat by Joe's side as he endured soul-wrenching withdrawal from GHB. Finally, there was Kevin Torvik, a man who had refused to give up on Joe.

His progress was painfully slow, but everyone who knew Joe saw that his resolution had returned. There was no boundary on earth that was going to stop him from beating the vice-grip of addiction, no devil powerful enough to force him to "tap out."

His friend Jimmy told Joe that God had a plan for him, though neither could have known at the time what that plan might be. Even today, Joe focuses less on outcome than he does on process—his daily interactions with people from all walks of life. "Outcomes look after themselves," he says. "I am responsible for the journey that gets me to those points."

The journey ahead of him would be long and hard, but he basked in the fact that he had already made the most important move of all. He had taken the first step.

11

VISITORS came and went. Family members were the most attentive, along with Joe's old friends. Most of the brotherhood that Joe had aspired so desperately to be part of was noticeable by its absence. Whether it was because he was now viewed as a fallen Angel, whether it was out of concern that Joe would be under police surveillance or whether it was because they simply had more pressing issues to attend to, they were nowhere to be seen.

The healing process was slow and laborious. Joe ingested liquids designed to provide a filling and nutritious diet. Bad as this routine was of sucking breakfast, lunch and dinner through a straw, it was no worse, and certainly healthier, than most of the "meals" Joe had endured on the street.

Even more difficult than drinking was trying to speak. There was little or no mobility in Joe's jaw after it had been reset through surgery and the wire stabilizers had been removed. Nonetheless, what those close to him heard Joe say over and over, in a voice as determined as it was Godfather-like, was that he was starting life over again. No longer would he be ruled by forces that held him hostage. From now on, he'd be the one in control.

The pain in Joe's jaw would have finished many a lesser man.

Each day it asserted itself like an abscessed tooth times ten, an explosion that began in the centre of his jaw and radiated outward, reaching the mandible at one end and his chin at the other. Still, Joe declined relief. No drugs, period, legal or otherwise.

What Joe had that his street brothers and sisters frequently did not have was a family, in addition to a loyal coterie of friends who still cared. What he lacked, though, was a clear sense of what lay ahead. Would he be able to kick his habit, or would it eventually land him, like it had so many others, in the morgue? Would he be able to reconnect with the society he had turned his back on, or would he revert to a life of crime, a life where the risks were great but the rewards were greater? To Joe and those around him, these questions were as real and as frightening as the broken jaw from which he was struggling to recover. But deep within, Joe knew that his life was not to be cut short. Somehow, even in his periods of greatest darkness, he knew he would survive. His life held greater purpose.

Joe acknowledged that he was the architect of the misery he was now enduring. He understood that. But he also believed in a power greater than himself—greater than the wealth and fame his life of crime had brought him, greater than the drugs that had almost killed him, and greater than even the people who were closest to him and had helped save his life. In a word, that power was God.

Joe was not a frequent churchgoer, but deep inside him there existed a spiritual sense of the meaning of existence. He believed he was destined for something greater than merely acquiring wealth, prestige or power. He believed that God had a plan for him. That plan, still inchoate but starting to gain shape, would set Joe on the path to helping others.

God has a twisted sense of humour at times. I don't always get it; I don't claim to. But the journey that's unfolding before me has had these incredible moments, moments that remind me there is greater meaning—a greater sense of purpose—than mere coincidence.

————

Released from hospital, Joe returned to the comfort and support of his parents' home. While he lay in an upstairs bedroom in full recovery mode, his ex-wife Linda inhabited the basement suite below with their two boys. Joe's and Linda's paths rarely crossed, but knowing that Jo Jo and Luca were so close by brought Joe a sense of peace and fuelled his determination.

The Calendinos knew that Joe's recovery would be a mixture of positive strides and periodic backward steps. As the months passed and Joe secured his own residence in Chilliwack, the biggest difference they observed was in his behaviour: it was no longer unpredictable. When he said he would show up at the family home at a specific time, he did—traffic jams, Joe's nemesis, notwithstanding. When he told his family "Nothing but water to drink for me," he meant it. When he said he was getting better day by day, they believed him. Yes, there were setbacks, but Joe was definitely on an upward trajectory.

One person who noticed the difference in Joe and thought there might be something he could do to assist was his former drama teacher, Jim Crescenzo. Like many others, Jim had lost direct contact with Joe as Joe became more enmeshed in the Hells Angels. Unlike others, though, Jim knew from his multitude of sources what Joe was up to.

Jim was a deeply religious man whose own life had been characterized by challenge and change. He had lost his father at a young age, and a debilitating medical condition, Crohn's disease, sometimes had him writhing in pain. Jim was raising his own boys with his wife, Tina. While providing inspiration to countless young students, Jim was prepared to add one more item to his already full agenda: Joe Calendino. He knew that Joe's recovery would depend on the support of family and friends. Furthermore, he knew Joe could succeed only if he was able to find genuine purpose on his new life path. Jim resolved that he would be there to encourage Joe, to laugh with him, to cry and pray with him. He also resolved that he would help Joe go where he could make a difference in his own life while having an impact on the lives of others—working with at-risk youth.

Soon Joe was spending days on end at Templeton Secondary School, home to Jim and Vice-Principal Walter Mustapich's Boys' Club, a group for young men whose turbulent lives could very easily take them in the wrong direction. There was Van, a teenager whose uncle, a man who was like a father to him, had been shot and killed at close range. It hadn't taken long for Van's festering anger to find its outlet in a Vietnamese-based gang, where he became a feared enforcer. There was Dewa'an, a talented young rap artist who came from a single-parent family and whose mom struggled with serious issues of addiction. There was Kristoff, whose boyish features belied many years already riddled with drug abuse and criminal gang activity. These were boys whose lives had catapulted them prematurely into manhood and whose futures looked depressingly bleak. In the Boys' Club, they had a home and a base of support.

Joe spoke to the boys in terms they understood. He didn't mince words, dropping F-bombs as freely as teachers of English drop metaphors. He looked the students squarely in the eye when he told them the direction they were headed was filled not with girls, respect and glory, but with violence, intimidation and paranoia. Underlining his message was the roll call of young gangland casualties in the Lower Mainland: Bindy Johal, Sukh Dhak and Thomas Gisby among them.

There was no arguing Joe's point. Gang life had one of two outcomes, neither of them good: you either ended up dead or you lived a life in which you were in constant fear of ending up dead.

Joe was a natural at the work he was doing, and Crescenzo and Mustapich knew he could be a powerful force for change in reaching youth. On Joe's behalf, Jim arranged for a meeting with

Gary Little, Joe's former counsellor, who was by now an associate superintendent for the Vancouver South area of the VSB. Jimmy, Walter and Joe arrived right on time at Gary's office. It was years since Little had seen Joe and he was shocked by Joe's appearance. Joe was thin, almost skeletal, a far cry from the sinewy teen Little had known in their Templeton days. Joe's suit looked as if it had been borrowed from a much bigger friend, Little thought; it hung loosely on his frame. The bandage attached to Joe's neck to stem the seepage from his injury appeared ready to fall off at any minute. Despite all of that, Little found something reassuringly familiar about Joe.

Joe smiled easily, but his expression contained an awkwardness Little had never seen in him before. Jim and Walter did most of the talking; Joe listened, adding snippets here and there. Joe had already formed important bonds with the students through his volunteering, Mustapich and Crescenzo enthused. They believed in Joe and his ability to move the Boys' Club forward. That much was clear. It was equally clear that Joe had some distance to go with his health before he was ready to volunteer on a larger scale. His voice lacked clarity and robustness, in part because of the problem with his jaw. Mentally, he seemed ready for the tough road that lay ahead, but his physical presentation was that of a man who was not yet in fighting trim.

Gary Little realized that if Joe continued his recovery, he'd be able to do transformative things with the students he encountered. There were a couple of issues that needed to be addressed, though. First, Joe had to get better. That was a given. Second, if Joe and the Boys' Club model were to have any chance of school board support, they would have to scale up, in order to serve greater numbers of students. Vulnerable kids were found in schools in every part of the city, not to mention the country. How would Joe begin to reach even a fraction of them?

The meeting ended with several commitments and goodwill all round. Jim, Walter and Joe would continue to refine Joe's presentation, a necessary step if he was to receive endorsement from the Vancouver School Board. From Little's vantage point, the political risk was huge, and due diligence was a must. What school district in North America had ever given the green light to a former Hells Angel to work with the students in its care? Trustees would be the ones standing in front of the cameras if the initiative fell apart. They would need to be certain that Joe was ready.

The plan the four men agreed to propose to the Board of Trustees was simple: a healthy Joe would present to students in large groups, either in person or through media such as film or the Internet. Interested schools would follow up with a specific curriculum designed to allow teachers to probe in depth the topics Joe had raised. Students who required intensive one-to-one support would get it.

Other steps were discussed as well. The group agreed to involve Lisa Pedrini, manager of Social Responsibility and Diversity for the Vancouver School Board, in the development of the program. Pedrini not only brought tremendous expertise to her portfolio, she also had extensive contacts outside the school system who would be able to lend their support. Before any final decision was made, school board trustees, at least some of them, would also need to see Joe's work first-hand.

If he made up his mind to do it, Joe Calendino would be the best presenter on gang violence that Vancouver schools had ever seen. Mustapich and Crescenzo could not read Joe's mind as they left the school board building, but they could read his heart. Everything about his demeanour said he was up for the plan—"balls in," as Joe liked to say.

Little, mulling over what had just transpired in his office, considered the next steps. He decided he would talk to trustees Jane Bouey and Sharon Gregson, both of whom knew Templeton Secondary School intimately and would understand the need to have a presenter with street cred, someone at-risk, gang-vulnerable kids would respect and listen to. After hearing about the plan, Bouey and Gregson indicated their support in principle for Joe working with students in the Vancouver system. Like everyone else involved, though, they'd need to be certain that Joe was clean and sober, as well as capable, and that his association with the Hells Angels was truly behind him. That was essential to protect the teens who were in the school board's care.

Joe continued his work with the Templeton Boys' Club, enjoying by now the full support of the school's principal, first Chris Atkinson and later Ellen Roberts. Crescenzo and Mustapich also began coaching Joe on his presentation skills. His voice gained strength, and his delivery was increasingly fluid. His language was still punctuated by four-letter words, but these issued forth with less frequency. Joe's physical health continued to improve as well, due in large measure to a proper diet and a return to his beloved martial arts. The suits that had once hung loose on his emaciated frame now fit as they should—and not because they had been tailored in. Joe's muscles were regaining definition. His eyes no longer sat deep-set in their sockets as the ravages of cocaine use and sleep deprivation diminished. His jet-black hair, streaked with grey, was still long, but it was no longer greasy and unkempt.

Despite such obvious gains, Joe still had a long way to go. That became evident when he presented a rehearsed speech several weeks after the meeting in Gary Little's office to Trustee Bouey, Lisa Pedrini, Little and Alison Rowley, who was part of the Community Assessment and Action Network. The topic was Joe's personal battle with cocaine addiction, and his talk was intended as a kind of dry run.

Held at Templeton, the presentation did not go well. Trustee Gregson was unable to attend, meaning that even if Trustee Bouey was convinced Joe was on track and on message, there wouldn't be a second trustee to back up her perceptions. In addition, Joe was clearly still in the midst of recovery. The script was too close to him; he was unable to get through it. Emotion overwhelmed him.

Nevertheless, it was clear to the four invited guests that there was something both heart-wrenching and heart-warming about Joe. He was honest. He was committed. He was passionate. He wanted to make a difference in the lives of young people. While he was still not ready to hit Vancouver classrooms, prime time as it were, he was getting closer.

12

CRESCENZO and Mustapich were understandably disappointed that Joe's presentation had not gone better, but they knew that supporting Joe's efforts to work with the youth of Vancouver would be a process rather than a singular event. They redoubled their efforts.

Joe, somewhat shaky at first but gaining strength with every passing day, continued his volunteer work with the Boys' Club. Despite his improvement, he knew he was just getting started. His recovery from drug addiction was headed in the right direction, but he was also aware that without vigilance he could easily slide back to his old ways. And he knew his presentations, vastly improved over his initial attempts, needed further refinement if he was to achieve the level of professionalism he desired.

Fortune smiled on Joe in the form of his old school, BCIT. Contacts there heard about the work he was doing with younger students and offered him a fully funded seat in their communication program. Joe jumped at the opportunity.

He discovered that just as years had changed him, they had changed the school as he remembered it. For one thing, his classmates were much younger than he was. For another, they were a more eclectic group, drawn from a variety of businesses, not-for-profit organizations and public institutes.

One of the central components of the program was the development and delivery of presentations that were short on verbosity and long on punch. Each student was required to put together a set of PowerPoints connected to their business or goals. For Joe, deciding on the subject was easy. He wanted to develop a presentation that covered the key elements of his life and his new passion—helping youth make wise choices at critical junctures in their lives. As he had done elsewhere, he threw himself into the task, with some promising results. His draft presentations were no longer pedestrian; he felt they had begun to take on the polished look of someone who had been doing this for years.

Joe invited feedback from several of his classmates, including a young woman named Val Jacobson. She had recently been promoted to a management position at a company called Squirrel, which designed computing systems used widely in the restaurant sector. After Jacobson viewed one of Joe's efforts, she erupted with friendly laughter.

"Joe, I've heard all of this before," she told him. "No offence intended, but my mother has been doing this kind of stuff forever."

Joe was taken aback at first, but then he chuckled. "Perhaps your mom should be the one to give me some feedback, then. Do you think she might be prepared to take a look at my work and chat with me about it?"

"I'll have to let her be the judge of that," Jacobson replied, "but I'm happy to talk to her. I'll let you know what she says."

When Jacobson floated the idea past her mother, Brenda Frisse, Frisse was uncertain. Having been married to a police officer and now enjoying a career as a respected educator, she wasn't sure how close she wanted to get to a former Hells Angel. She didn't mind offering feedback online, but sitting down with

Joe to review his presentation was different. She wasn't convinced that would be a wise course of action. However, she did make one concession. She agreed she'd chat with Joe on the phone and see where things went from there.

Joe and Frisse set up a call, and she listened with growing interest to this man whose sincerity was evident over the line. Joe's cadences, his use of language and his straightforward "street" simplicity reminded Frisse of the neighbourhood in which she'd grown up and of the various characters who populated it. She felt herself being drawn back to the inner city of her youth.

Joe forwarded a couple of rough-draft presentations to Frisse. She reviewed them with her usual critical eye and passed along her feedback by email. At that point, there was nothing of a personal nature attached to the process, simply a professional interaction between two people—one trying to sharpen his communication skills, the other trying to help.

In one of Joe's emails, after letting Frisse know he'd be working in school districts to spread his message, he invited her to dinner. "It's a small thanks, but I would like to express my gratitude for all that you have done for me," he wrote.

Coming from some men, this would have been a rather feeble and fumbling pickup attempt. Coming from Joe, it resonated with sincerity. Frisse agreed—sort of. Rather than dinner, she thought it best they meet at her local Starbucks. That would be thanks enough, and it was a public place where she'd be under no sense of obligation and no pressure.

Frisse waited at a small table outside the coffee shop with thoughts racing through her mind. Why had she said yes to this guy? What if she disliked him? How would she disengage herself from the situation if need be? On the other hand, what if she actually liked him? How might this play out? After a few minutes, she became aware of the insistent tone of the phone ringing in her purse. She grabbed it. The name on the call display was Joe Calendino.

From her vantage point in front of Starbucks, Frisse watched a car pull into the parking lot and a man get out. He was as different from the typical suburban Starbucks customer as fish are from fowl: hair down past his shoulders, a black T-shirt with some indecipherable script on it, black Daytons and rumpled blue jeans. He certainly was not trying to dazzle anyone with a Gucci wardrobe. Frisse could see the man had a cell phone cradled against his ear.

"Brenda. It's Joe. I'm running a few minutes late, but I'll be right there. Traffic has been brutal."

"Not a problem," said Frisse. "Take your time. See you shortly."

"Oh shoot," she thought to herself, "that's him. Maybe I should just get up and walk away. Probably too late, though. He's probably already seen me and is getting ready to walk up to me and say, 'Hi, you must be Brenda.' Maybe I should just tell him 'Sorry, you have the wrong person' and highball it out of here."

"It was the Italian thing," Brenda Frisse says today, "the cocky attitude and swagger that he presented. I remember thinking at that moment, 'A smart woman would get up and leave.' I guess I wasn't so smart; I just sat there, frozen. He walked over to me. 'You're Val's mom?' I really did contemplate saying no, but he immediately told me that I looked just like Val. I realized, 'I'm done.'"

Frisse answered, "I *am* Val's mom," and those four words kicked off a long, breezy conversation. As it turned out, Joe and Brenda had many friends and acquaintances in common. They came from similar backgrounds. They talked about the people they knew, one after another—that six degrees of separation thing.

It's been said by some that a fine line distinguishes the criminal from the cop. Cops and criminals frequently grow up in similar circumstances—they're working-class kids who aspire to something greater. They often have a strong sense of family, meaning they're attracted to the brotherhood of the gang or the camaraderie of the police force. Some of the people Brenda and Joe discussed had moved in a lawless direction. Some had gone the opposite way, committing to uphold the law.

It didn't take long for Brenda to realize there was something else at play here. Growing up, she wouldn't have given two seconds to a guy like Joe. She found the mentality of anyone who needed to be a member of a gang off-putting. But the man in front of her didn't fit her stereotype.

"Here's this guy sitting in front of me," she recalls, "this caring, compassionate and gentle man. And he had done what? There was this real curiosity in me where I tried to reconcile the two, the stereotypical image I had of gang members with this individual who had been at the apex of the gang hierarchy."

Joe told Brenda about the work he was doing and his dreams of expanding it. Frisse was captivated. She had recently moved from front-line work to a management position in her school district. She worried she had left the intensity of the playing field for a position on the bench, where she was required to oversee and direct the players, not play the game itself.

"I had lost that first-hand experience," she says. "Hearing Joe speak about it reignited that passion in me. 'What am I doing in the board office?' I thought. 'I want to roll up my sleeves and be back out there—making a direct difference.' His passion was contagious."

Their coffee long ago drained from their cups, the two of them ended their conversation. They would connect in the near future, they agreed. No agenda. No plan. Just a commitment to get together. For Joe, the change he was about to experience was a door to the future. For Brenda, it represented a door to the past. She loved her work in the school district, but she knew in her heart it was time to make a change, a profound change that would take her back to the place she'd come from. Of course, it wouldn't be simple for either of them.

"Joe still needed to come to terms with his past and be okay with it," Brenda explains. "What's done is done. You can't undo it by putting on blinders and saying it didn't exist. Yes it did. There are some wonderful things as a result of that—four beautiful children, for instance. By my looking at the past, our shared neighbourhood, with excitement, Joe was able to see it through that lens as well."

From their opening handshake, Brenda and Joe knew that somehow their lives fit together. They were not teens in love. Both had been through the wars, figuratively speaking. They were two adults in mid-life who had been thrust together by circumstances, and to both of them, it seemed meant to be.

BRENDA DECIDED TO help Joe in the best way she could: by working with him on the presentations he would make to members of the Boys' Club and, in time, elsewhere. That also meant helping Joe develop a firm philosophical foundation on which to base his work.

One of the club's activities was hosting members of the community who had successfully overcome some of the same challenges these young East End men faced: financial hardships, family dysfunction, violence and insecurity. The speakers were high-flying financiers, movie moguls and even the owner of Vancouver's professional hockey team, the Canucks. Their poise and confidence were an inspiration. Joe sat in on these sessions whenever possible, absorbing the life lessons and also the manner in which they were delivered. Sometimes, his respect for the presenters clouded his better judgment, he recalls. At least that was the case on one occasion.

One day I made my way to the high school, and when I got there I found out that one of the kids I had been working with had had a family tragedy. One of his family members had killed himself. This kid—he was my favourite student.

The speaker that day was from a very powerful family. The kid walked in late. He walked straight toward me. I could see the pain in his face. I gave him a reassuring hug and whispered to him that we would talk later. That was wrong of me! He needed my attention right then and there. I should have excused myself, taken the young man with me and had a good one-on-one conversation somewhere outside. I could see he was in a place I have frequented too many times in my own life. He was experiencing a pain so deep that it required immediate attention. He needed me then, not five minutes or half an hour later. He needed me right then.

Unfortunately, politeness got the better of me. I thought it could wait until the speaker was done. I was wrong.

———

Joe grew stronger, gaining confidence. On one occasion, after a Boys' Club session, he stood talking to Jim Crescenzo, tears spilling from his dark eyes. Crescenzo was worried. "Is everything all right, bro?" he asked Joe. "I know we've had a couple of tough ones lately, but you're doing a great job. You're making progress. I don't want you getting down on yourself."

A smile broke across Joe's face. "Not at all, Jimmy. These aren't tears of pain. They're tears of joy. I've never been happier in my life."

The students Joe worked with knew that this man who had entered their lives was happy. They could see it in his face, in his every action. They knew as well that he was committed to them and to their own successes, however they defined them— as long as those successes were not gang-based. Joe shared with the students his very personal thoughts on gang life, a narrative that was becoming more finely tuned with each telling. He drew on the inspiring film *Coach Carter*, based on the true story of a California high school basketball coach named Ken Carter. Joe often quoted Timo Cruz, one of Carter's proteges, whose insight serves as motivation for Joe.

Our deepest fear is not that we are inadequate. Our deepest fear is that we are powerful beyond measure. It is our light, not our darkness, that most frightens us.

Your playing small does not serve the world. There is nothing enlightened about shrinking so that other people won't feel insecure around you. We were all meant to shine, as children do.

It's not just in some of us; it's in everyone, and as we let our own light shine we unconsciously give people permission to do the same as we are liberated from our own fear. Our presence automatically liberates others.

Sir, I just want to say thank you. You saved my life.

Students sat spellbound as Joe recounted his entry into the most dangerous recesses of gang life, his harrowing descent into cocaine addiction and the redemption he'd attained by getting clean. The values prized in gang life couldn't be more different from those espoused by Coach Carter, he told them.

———

In gang life, that's how things work—darkness toward others. The ability to be without remorse or guilt for your actions will never be questioned; in fact, the opposite is true. More often than not you are rewarded. Showing empathy or compassion is off limits. To say something like "Let's not go five guys against one because that's too much—it's unfair" will just attract others' darkness toward you. To present your own light is usually looked at negatively, unfortunately.

———

Brenda Frisse attended a couple of Joe's presentations in Surrey and Vancouver, and she saw at once the impact Joe had on a school audience. Students listened. They leaned forward in their chairs. They understood what she too saw—that here was a guy who had not only been there and done that, but also believed in a better way for himself and the students he came into contact with. He couldn't guarantee them a better life; that depended on their own level of commitment. He could, however, guide them toward that better life with every fibre of his being. That was the promise he made.

Brenda and Joe found other ways to work together as well. At a workshop she led with a group of school counsellors, Brenda introduced the session by sharing part of Joe's story, then asked participants to predict how the story would end. The counsellors worked in small groups to develop their scripts. Brenda called a break in the activity—time for lunch. When they returned, she reassembled the participants into their groups—and in walked Joe.

Audible gasps filled the room. This was not the guy they'd expected based on the information Brenda had provided: the high school fighter, the BCIT grad who had run a successful business, the gang member who'd associated with some of the biggest and baddest dudes in British Columbia, the druggie who was sinking deeper by the day. This was not the outcome any of them had predicted, this man who addressed them with confidence, in good health and flashing an easy smile. They thought Joe would be dead maybe. In rehab, possibly. Homeless, very likely. But certainly not the Joe who now stood in front of them.

Joe addressed the group, showing them old photos of himself wearing his patch. He described the journey that had brought him to this point, omitting details he felt were either too incriminating or too salacious. The counsellors drank it in. Joe was the embodiment of the hope that drove their work.

Today, Brenda sums up her relationship with Joe in a single word: trust. She doesn't know all the details of his previous life, nor does she care to. She understands that Joe was a successful Hells Angel, one of the "one percenters," but she is not interested in exploring the details of that time. What happened happened. It shaped Joe into who he became. That life is behind him, and Brenda trusts him when he tells her that.

As a teacher of alternative education, Brenda shaped lives. She helped youth on the margins of school society believe in themselves and in their futures. She was good at what she did, but when she met Joe she was already wondering how she might positively influence young peoples' lives in greater numbers. Initially, with a career shift into counselling and eventually into a school district position, she'd seen new possibilities. But while her reach had extended, the direct impact she was able to have on students had diminished. In Joe, she saw the perfect vehicle for remedying that. Whereas many presenters simply tell their story, then move on to the next school or venue, Joe's approach was different. Brenda could see that, with her support and understanding of school systems, they could utilize various tiers, ensuring that students who needed modest support received it, and that those who required more intensive support got that as well. With that realization, a remarkable partnership was born.

13

AT Templeton Secondary School, Jim Crescenzo and Walter Mustapich continued their work of supporting Joe. One of the ideas they landed on was a play based on Joe's life—its ascents and descents and his ultimate redemption. The play would serve as a springboard to discussion, they thought, not only about Joe's place in the public schools but about the importance of these issues in the larger sphere. They enlisted the talents of Peter Grasso, a playwright and former student of Crescenzo's who had carved out a place for himself in Vancouver's theatre scene.

Grasso approached the task with his usual professionalism, honoured to be included in the project. He researched Joe's life with painstaking care, interviewing family members, friends and Joe himself. His play focused on the lows and the highs Joe had experienced: his criminal activities, his attraction into the seductive world of drugs, his "bottoming out" and his remarkable recovery and transformation.

A production of Peter Grasso's paean to Joe, *Let Me Up*, was mounted by Mustapich and Crescenzo at Templeton High School in December 2010. The play stirred broad interest throughout the community. Reporter John Colbourne of the Vancouver *Province* newspaper described it as gritty and thought-provoking.

The play featured professional actors and a professional crew, supplemented by a few of Crescenzo's high school theatre students. The result was a poignant experience for the audience. On opening night, at least one audience member was moved to tears. Joe's mother, Nerina, stood on stage alongside the cast members who were enjoying the audience applause. Tears streaming down her face, she exulted, "Thank God I have my son back."

The audience included Vancouver cops, school and school board personnel, and even a member of the Hells Angels, according to Kevin Torvik, who recognized the biker from his work with the Outlaw Motorcycle Gang Unit. Most people came to see what was in the play. According to Torvik, one audience member had come to be sure of what was *not* in it. The school board professionals were impressed with the play, as were the police. Even the lone Hells Angel in attendance appeared to be satisfied. Joe was not the least bit interested in exposing that part of his life for the prurient enjoyment of anyone. He was not, as he said sneeringly of the undercover VPD agent who had infiltrated the East End chapter of the Angels, a "rat." If anyone expected otherwise, they left the theatre disappointed.

The play was a solid launch pad for further presentations, discussion and curriculum development. Joe's confidence had grown with the passage of time and with his various successes. He was brash, as always, yet soulful and reflective. He had even regained the strut he'd exhibited years earlier in the hallways of Templeton Secondary. He didn't pull any punches with the students in the Boys' Club either. "You want to travel down this journey? You really want to travel down this journey? I'll explain this journey to you, no problem. I'll take you there. I've been shot at. I've been stabbed. I've been run over. I have lived the gang life, and I'm grateful to be able to stand before you and blow apart its myths, piece by bloody piece," Joe challenged one group. He raised his right hand and pulled the trigger on an imaginary gun.

"Is this tough?" he questioned. "Is this what makes a man? This isn't tough. What is tough? I ask you."

Joe turned his back to the students, stroking his hair while he awaited their responses.

"Tough is being able to back your talk with your actions," said one student.

"Tough is walking away from a fight even when you know you can beat the shit out of the other guy," said another.

"Tough is facing life's challenges and not bending," said a third.

Joe smiled and turned around to face the students. He knew from bitter experience that all of these answers were correct—to a point. He felt his message was getting through. No one had said that tough was leading a gang. No one had said that tough was pumping bullets into another human being. No one had said that tough was being the biggest, baddest badass on the block.

Joe was not interested in labels. He didn't care if a young man was defined by the school system as being at risk, whether he came from a family that was dysfunctional, whether he was a drug user. He didn't care what minority group—if any—the boy belonged to. All Joe cared about was whether the young man in question was serious about fashioning a better life for himself.

———

If a kid is already in a gang, it is sometimes too late. But if I can see he's sincere in changing his life and freeing himself from the clutches of the gang, then there is something we can work with. I won't quit on the kid. Ever.

Of course, school boards don't always want to hear that. They don't want to hear that gang members frequent their

hallways—who would?—so one has to tread carefully. Help the
student, by all means, but don't put the fact he may have gang
ties in large letters on the school's electronic messaging board.
Be respectful of his privacy, but be firm in letting the student
know there's no such thing as "sort of" getting out of a gang.
Either you are sincere or you are not. You leave the gang or you
don't. There is no halfway house. I need to know that at some level
the young man is truly committed to turning his life around—
that he wants a better life than he will ever get in a gang.

———

Membership in the Boys' Club typically fluctuated between ten
and fifteen students. Their attendance and achievements were
monitored, their daily challenges and successes discussed. The
young men looked not only behind to what had been in their lives
but also ahead to what could be. Joe was instrumental in helping
them shape their visions. He discussed with them the duality of
life: good and evil, success and failure, contentment and disappointment. They talked about the real issues of life and death.

Progress for students in the club was not always observ-
able. It was certainly not linear. Strides were never measured
in steady increments. Some kids seemed to make critically
important changes in their lives quickly. Others took longer.

There was Vince, a young man who, like Joe, had been kicked
out of his neighbourhood high school. Vince ended up at Templeton, and through the work of Mustapich and Crescenzo got
connected to Joe and the Boys' Club. Never a good student, as he
himself acknowledged, Vince began attending school on a full-
time basis, committed to his studies and today is well on track
to securing qualification in a post-secondary trades program.
His parents, frequently at odds with their son, were joyful and
incredulous at the transformation they observed.

"I owe it to Joe, and I owe it to the Boys' Club," Vince says
with great animation. "Even my parents are shocked at how

well things are going. I can't wait to graduate and get a trade, a good job."

Van took longer to turn things around. At first he studied intently the goings-on of the Boys' Club.

"I just kind of sat back and observed for what was probably weeks on end," he says. "When my uncle was shot in the head, I kind of lost trust in the human race. It took a long time to get it back. I could not believe how open Joe was, and how accepting he was of everyone in the group. It took me longer than most to realize that this guy is the real deal."

Van explains the role he took on in the world of gangs after the death of his uncle. "I was sort of their enforcer. If we were owed money, I made sure we got it. If a supply of drugs went missing, I would determine the cause, identify the culprit and make sure that we were repaid—with interest. I was angry. I trusted no one. Why should I? I had lost the man I loved more than anyone else in the world and for no reason at all, a bullet lodged deep inside his brain."

Van is articulate, soft-spoken and reflective. It's easy to imagine him becoming a successful professional, a lawyer, perhaps, or a business executive. He won't be returning to a life of crime, he says. According to Van, that's the power Joe has had on his life.

Another event of consequence for Joe occurred during this time. Kevin Torvik was familiar with the Odd Squad, an assemblage of Vancouver Police Department members and civilians who were determined to help steer vulnerable individuals in society away from crime and addiction. They did so through the medium of film, creations such as the hard-hitting and gritty *Tears for April—Beyond the Blue Lens*, a look at addiction in Vancouver's Downtown Eastside. Joe, Torvik reasoned, would fit perfectly into the work that this not-for-profit organization did. He connected Joe to Toby Hinton and Brian Shipper, two pivotal Odd Squad figures.

Hinton and Shipper began filming shortly after they met Joe. The two men knew a good story when they saw one—and Joe definitely was a good story, particularly when shot against the backdrop of the Boys' Club and the young men for whom the club was making a difference.

Another person ready to take a chance on Joe was Rob Rothwell. He had been the VPD's school liaison officer at Templeton Secondary while Joe was a student there, and he'd always seen something special in Joe.

"Joe treated me with respect when we were at Templeton," Rothwell recalls, "and I always admired that in him. He understood what my role was and listened respectfully when I had to speak to him. Truth be told, he was almost like a caricature of an East End tough kid at the time—he reminded me of one of those kids you see in the old TV series *Welcome Back, Kotter*. That's the high school part of it, where we first connected. It really is strange the way our lives play out."

From there, Rothwell jumps ahead in his narrative. "I knew the Joe that existed within that rough, tough exterior. I knew the Joe that wasn't the biker, the sincerity that he possessed, the integrity that existed within his being. I did not endorse his lifestyle, for sure. In fact, I hated his lifestyle. I even led investigations to charge him with criminal offences that were part of that lifestyle. Of course, everybody has some level of suspicion when it comes to individuals like Joe who say they're about to turn their lives around—a natural reluctance to commit too much in case it all turns out to be not true. You don't want to make a poor decision, to be hoodwinked in some manner.

"Frankly, given the relationship between cops and bikers, there is not a bridge anywhere that will ever be substantial enough to span that gap. There's so much distrust between the two groups, complete revulsion, in fact. In general, the cops perceived Joe as being a complete asshole. He did a lot of what

I would call asshole things. So while I was prepared to support his work with youth—cautiously, I might add—I wasn't surprised that many others were disbelieving or took a wait-and-see approach."

SEEING PETER GRASSO'S play did convince school staff and administrators that Joe had something special to offer. Lisa Pedrini and others in the Vancouver School District scoured their own meagre budgets and external sources such as Youth Gang Prevention to secure the necessary funding. Surrey had already jumped in with both feet, thanks to the connections made by Jim Crescenzo and Walter Mustapich. Theresa Campbell, from Surrey Safe Schools, led the way, supported in significant measure by Rob Rai, who later replaced Campbell as manager of this valued service.

Surrey Safe Schools oversees the Wrap Program, described in a brochure as an anti-gang initiative "delivering services to youth who exhibit signs of gang-associated behaviour." The program derives its name from its "wrap-around" philosophy, which combines the knowledge and skills necessary for positive pathways in life with a 360-degree support network. The students who enter the program do so by referral. They are not necessarily gang-connected—at least not yet. The concern is that they soon will be, if they don't discover a better alternative to their current lifestyle. It was a philosophy that fit perfectly with Joe's message and his own life experience.

Joe was not yet ready to work on his own, at least not in the estimation of Theresa Campbell and others. But he was determined. He studied others who made presentations to youth. He learned what separated effective presentations from those that failed to resonate. He learned the art of pacing, of taking time to ensure that students had a chance to voice their concerns and get their questions answered. He learned that his story was what students wanted to hear, not some canned presentation pulled from the shelf.

At long last, Joe signed a contract with Surrey Safe Schools, and his first real paycheque for doing this kind of work soon followed. Even he found it hard to believe that the dream he'd had while lying on a concrete floor in a cold jail cell had come to fruition. He'd never felt more fulfilled and more alive. He needed money to live on, especially with children to support, but a paycheque was never his primary motivation for doing what he did. His motivation was making a difference for the youth he served.

Lisa Pedrini had done pivotal work for the Vancouver School District in creating safer schools. Following horrific school tragedies such as that at Columbine High School in Littleton, Colorado, Pedrini worked with Kevin Cameron, a noted Canadian expert, on how best to ensure Vancouver schools did not fall prey to a similar horror. She worked with respected researchers Shelley Hymel and Kim Schonert-Reichl of the University of British Columbia to better understand student attitudes toward safety, inclusivity and social responsibility, and to learn how to use this information in the most effective way possible: prevention. She did important liaison work with the Vancouver Police Department, helping to ensure that the district's respected School Liaison Program continued to enjoy the support of both the Vancouver School Board and the Vancouver Police Department. Pedrini felt Joe had proved his readiness, and she was squarely behind bringing him into Vancouver schools. She offered him the chance to give another mock presentation, this time to a group of students and teachers.

The first thing that struck Pedrini was the remarkable improvement in Joe. His voice resonated with clarity. He no longer slouched; his shoulders were square to the audience, his posture upright. His eyes flashed with confidence and passion. The second thing Pedrini noticed was that Joe was right on message. He had always been a no-nonsense kind of guy. That hadn't changed. But now he exhibited a good sense of how to adjust his presentation for different audiences and different contexts. The third thing she noted was the reaction of the audience. Young or old, the people who heard him speak identified with Joe.

That day, Pedrini saw what everyone else saw too. She saw that Joe could empower others. She made a commitment then and there that she would do whatever she could to help find a place for Joe in Vancouver schools. She needed political support. That wasn't a problem. By now, both trustees and senior management were on side. She also needed some way of addressing Joe's criminal past. Any employee who'd be working with students was required to undergo a criminal records check, and the person was disqualified if it came up positive. The whole world knew how Joe would score on such a test: with a big fat F. Then there was the issue of his addiction. Was he still using, even if it was just sneaking the occasional line of cocaine? There was no room for error. Pedrini had to be sure. The answer had to be an unequivocal no.

The criminal part was easy to solve, in fact. Joe would be required to work alongside a professional member of the school staff whenever he was with students. There could be no compromise on this arrangement; he'd be like a student-teacher, only more so, under direct supervision at all times. Pedrini knew that if there was ever an allegation something untoward had happened in a classroom and involving Joe, and it turned out he'd been alone with students at the time, there would be hell to pay—for Joe, for her and for the entire Vancouver school system.

The drug use issue was a little trickier. There had been cases in Vancouver public schools where employees were required to submit to mandatory drug or alcohol testing as part of their continued employment, but these were rare, and they involved only contract personnel. How could Joe, still a volunteer at that time, be required to submit to drug testing? And who would be responsible for picking up the tab if he agreed to the testing, given the fact he was not on the Vancouver School Board payroll?

Fortunately, Vancouver School Board staff came up with the answer. Joe's work with students was too important to let the cost of drug testing be a deal breaker. It was a necessary part of doing business, and the meagre amount of money involved was soon found. Joe not only agreed to mandatory drug testing but decided to use it as a motivator for students. If he could stay off drugs, he reasoned, so could they.

ONCE JOE'S WORK in the schools began, officially sanctioned thanks to the efforts of Lisa Pedrini and built on a solid curriculum developed by Brenda Frisse, interest in it escalated. However, most of the inquiries were still directed not to Pedrini but to Mustapich, Crescenzo and the Templeton's Boys' Club. Mustapich and Crescenzo were actively putting out feelers, forwarding information to local media to publicize the story they personally found so compelling. Cover stories in publications such as the *Province*, British Columbia's second-largest newspaper, got the word out. Joe's mission was well underway.

Joe knew he could not achieve on his own the goals he'd set for himself. If he was really to help change young people's lives, it could not be done one life at a time. He was determined to imbue his larger presentations with the same nuance and profundity as his one-to-one interactions.

How to go about doing this, though? Everyone seemed to have a different answer, something Joe found increasingly unsettling. Crescenzo and Mustapich outlined one potential route to "scalability" through careful and considered use of media: newspaper articles, radio shows, television appearances—even the possibility of a full-length movie based on Joe's life story. The rest, they believed, would follow. Presentations before jam-packed auditoriums of high school students. Theatres overflowing with audiences of all ages interested in Joe's story—that kind of thing. Maybe even an appearance on *Oprah*, whose show was at the peak of popularity in those days.

There were others who held a somewhat different view, including Lisa Pedrini, Gary Little and Brenda Frisse. They felt Joe's work would have the most impact if scaled directly through the school system. Schools, they reasoned, offered richer and longer-lasting opportunities to reach young people. As Pedrini explains, "Schools hold connections that do not exist elsewhere. Joe provided a way of reaching students who do not easily connect with your average teacher or administrator. Furthermore, it showed these kids that the school did care about them."

Pedrini, Frisse and Little envisaged presentations where Joe would take centre stage, followed by in-class discussion. For deep and meaningful change to occur, they reasoned, teachers and counsellors were a necessary part of the picture. They'd play an important role in implementing a follow-up curriculum focused on helping youth build the skills and tools to deal with life. There was only one small problem with this model: the curriculum was not yet fully developed.

Successful delivery models are rarely an either-or proposition. They are usually a both-and affair. Mass media approaches are not incompatible with in-school programs. The broader the reach of most messages, the better. The more depth to the follow-up, the better still. But rightly or wrongly, Joe was developing serious misgivings about the mass media approach. The media attention he'd been getting was validating, at times exhilarating. Still, he felt in his heart that much more was needed. He had concerns that he was becoming the story rather than the catalyst for what he wanted the story to achieve—helping young people turn their lives around. He knew his background would command interest, and talking about it was necessary to shed important light on his message, but he also knew that there was a fine line between empowering youth and becoming the celebrity flavour of the day. He sensed he was in danger of crossing that line. No matter how powerful, one-shot presentations rarely promulgate lasting change. No matter how compellingly Joe could deliver his story, his audience required follow-up experiences that rooted his message in their own lives and decisions to make it enduring. The power to change resided in each individual, not in Joe.

Then there was Joe's relationship with the Odd Squad. Some of its members were steering Joe in yet another direction, toward a documentary that would capture his story with the grittiness of the productions they'd previously produced. An interesting idea, Joe thought, but merely one plank in a larger program that was not yet developed.

Joe's head was spinning. Increasingly, he felt as if he'd given up one kind of stressful existence only to replace it with another. There were days he would have been happy to jump aboard his Harley and keep riding to wherever the road led him.

In the midst of the cacophony were the people closest to him, most importantly Brenda, who kept reminding him, "Remember why you decided to do what you do—to make a positive difference for kids. Follow your heart, Joe. Keep true to your mission, and you will never go too far astray."

In the end, following his heart led Joe to sever his business ties with Crescenzo and Mustapich. It wasn't an easy decision. Jim and Walter had been instrumental in helping Joe get to where he was, and he would always be grateful for that. But the issue had become exceedingly clear in his mind. He needed to go in a different direction. It was that simple. After much deliberation, he'd landed on a trajectory that was deliberately modest: a program he and Brenda would construct for youth that was predicated on incremental growth.

There was no formal cessation of Joe's involvement in the Boys' Club, no contractual cutting of the ties. The Boys' Club continues to flourish, and it possesses a school focus not only in Vancouver's Templeton Secondary School but also in North Vancouver, where Walter serves as a vice-principal. In addition, he now heads the Boys' Club organization. At the club, various supporters drawn from throughout greater Vancouver share their stories with vulnerable youth. Through that kind of influence, as well as the connections they have with other boys in the group, these young men have a good chance at eschewing gang life forever and leading productive, ethical lives.

Following his decision, Joe ramped up his work in Surrey at schools like Queen Elizabeth and in Vancouver at Britannia Secondary. Funding from both districts was testament to the effect his influence was having. He and Brenda continued to discuss how a broader-based schools program might be developed, and Joe began to enlist the services of men and women who could serve as effective role models. Al Arsenault and Toby Hinton, pivotal members of the Odd Squad and respected VPD constables, were willing to give freely of their time to assist. So was Brian Shipper, a producer with the Odd Squad. Others too numerous to mention supported Joe and the work he was doing. What was clear to all these people was that something special was evolving.

14

I T was no surprise that when a name had to be adopted for the fledgling organization that was Joe supported by Brenda supported by others, Joe adopted Yo Bro. It was, after all, his signature greeting and his signature goodbye.

Yo Bro was Joe Calendino and the team that he and Brenda assembled. The program under development fit with Joe's philosophy that through care and compassion, people can make a difference. Yo Bro fit with his background. The organization's name was short and to the point, no BS. Yo Bro was not conceived as a save-the-world project with a catchy acronym and a network of ephemeral political backers. It was never intended as a panacea. It began simply with one person doing what he did best with the deepest commitment he could muster. Joe and Brenda set about creating a management team and a board of directors with the same deliberateness they brought to all their work together. A network of associated supporters also began to form.

Brenda had provided Joe with valuable early guidance on how to present his message with authenticity, professionalism and poise. Now she became the chief architect of the Yo Bro program's three components: Joe's presentation, the accompanying curriculum and one-to-one counselling follow-up. She provided a vital link to school systems for Joe, an entry into a world as foreign to him as the world of biker gangs was to Brenda. She also brought a creative edge to their endeavours that heightened their appeal.

Very soon, the decision was made that Yo Bro would not be just about boys and the problems they face entering adulthood. It would also be about young women and their equally compelling need for support and empowerment. Today, the organization is called the Yo Bro Yo Girl Youth Initiative.

Yo Bro Yo Girl borrows rhetoric and concepts from the two fields with which the organization is most closely affiliated: education and counselling. Its stated mission is "to engage at-risk youth in their schools and communities so they attain the skills and values necessary to realize their educational and career potential and contribute to the safety and well-being of their communities."

Teachers and school counsellors, supported by social workers, police officers and community youth workers, bring the requisite skills and training to build on Joe's story and YBYG's mission. Most importantly, their day-to-day work allows them to develop the relationships crucial to achieving success with the students they are trying to reach. Quiet support for YBYG has also come from some unexpected quarters. As Kevin Torvik is quick to remind everyone who cares to listen, "No gangster ever wants his kid to end up where he has ended up. That's why they are quite happy that Joe's doing the work he's doing."

There are three parts to the Yo Bro Yo Girl approach:

1 **The message:** Wherever possible, Joe initiates the program with a live address to students, followed by a Q and A. While

no two sessions are exactly the same, Joe is as firmly rooted in the message he imparts as a Douglas fir is in a west-coast storm. He treats all groups with respect, and he expresses the heartfelt hope that his story will make a difference to them—if not immediately, then in a pivotal moment before their lives spiral out of control. By deglamourizing gang life and speaking openly about his own struggles and mistakes, Joe instills hope in the youth who hear him speak, stripping away the veneer of glitz and glamour to reveal its ugly underbelly. If he could overcome the challenges he faced, he tells students, they can overcome the challenges they face.

2 **The hands-on work:** Joe's martial arts training has been of significant value to him throughout his journey. Through martial arts, he's developed inner strength and self-discipline coupled with an abiding belief in himself and others. Compassion is also a central tenet common to great martial arts teachers. Through the YBYG offerings, Joe and a group of selected staff and volunteers use their own training in martial arts to build connections with young men and women. When you get down on the mat with others, you enter a world that's founded on mutual respect, overcoming fears and building confidence. Joe and the other YBYG instructors impress these points on students in a safe, no-blows-to-the-head environment, committed as much to the mental aspects of the discipline—respect, self-control and spirituality—as they are to the physical side of the sport.

3 **The bureaucracy:** Since its founding, the Yo Bro Yo Girl Youth Initiative has maintained a dynamic board of directors to champion the YBYG cause and to help strengthen the organization and deepen its impact.

   As demand accelerates for the ten-week YBYG curriculum, technologies like podcasting, interactive videos and online streaming may sometimes have to take the place of Joe's live presentations. For the time being, however, Lesson One consists of the live component, with other resources providing useful follow-up. In Lessons Two and Three, grainy PowerPoint slides introduce Joe's family to the student audience. Subsequent lessons include a screening of the trailer for *Not Your Average Joe*, the Odd Squad production chronicling Joe's transition from successful businessman to gang-life major-domo to disgraced drug user, along with a gut-level look at the realities of gang life. What Joe makes clear is that real gang life is so rife with paranoia, threats and violence that even if you have the trappings of success, you rarely have the time or serenity to enjoy them.

No curriculum designed to help students make positive life choices would be complete without a section on asset building. By engaging students in a fearless and honest discussion of their own strengths, the facilitators of Taking It to the Streets do the most important work of all: they help students understand that they have the potential to achieve rich, rewarding and sustainable lives by being who they are and developing their talents. Students conclude the Taking It to the Streets program by mapping their futures. What are their goals? How will they achieve them? Who will help them in their quest? And how will they deal with adversity, a given in their lives, as it is in the lives of everyone?

The other prevention programs offered by YBYG to date include:

Respectful Relationships: A ten-week violence awareness and prevention program for boys and girls.

KNOW Means NO: YBYG's signature program for girls, addressing issues of violence against girls and women.

Street Safe: An ongoing program throughout the school year for elementary school students interested in building physical and mental strength under the tutelage of senior YBYG mentors.

Empowering Young Women: A second ten-week offering for girls only, designed to raise self-awareness, encourage self-empowerment and teach personal safety.

For students requiring more intensive counselling, Bro 4 Bro and Girl 2 Girl offer support individually or in small groups, as appropriate. To date, Joe and Brenda have provided this service to students, some of whom have addiction issues requiring help, others who have deeply rooted concerns about how to say no to those trying to coerce them into joining a gang. Some of the students struggle with life's daily challenges and need to talk to someone who cares. Whatever the case, Joe makes it abundantly clear that he is there for them. Even students who no longer have any formal connection to Yo Bro Yo Girl frequently call to seek his advice and support.

Some argue that Joe, unlike Brenda, is not a trained counsellor, and that this kind of counselling is best left to the pros. These are often the same people who argue that peer-based models cannot possibly succeed. As we know, though, for many people, models like Alcoholics Anonymous, Narcotics Anonymous and the myriad offshoots do work. Joe knows first-hand that of which he speaks. He knows what to say and when to say it, and he's attuned to danger signs that others sometimes miss when helping students. Young people trust Joe, plain and simple.

AT BRITANNIA SECONDARY, a typical YBYG after-school session begins with students gathered from Vancouver's east side. The young men and women live for the most part in the community immediately surrounding Britannia. A smattering of others arrive by bus from several miles away, motivated by the value they find in the program's components and by the relationships they have formed there. Not only do they receive the benefits of Joe's street-hardened wisdom, they learn skills that provide a positive alternative to gangs. The martial arts component of the program is heavy on the arts and light on the martial. Students discover its philosophical underpinnings: self-discipline, stress management, respect for others, patience and determination. They learn the importance of good health—not just optimal physical health gained through vigorous workouts and good diet but also psychological and spiritual well-being. They learn what it means to belong to a group whose importance supersedes that of any one member but at the same time values the uniqueness of each individual.

In keeping with the key constructs of Yo Bro Yo Girl, Joe and his co-instructors emphasize a number of "assets" for youth in their work.

First and most important is *self-respect*. Many of the students in YBYG have endured more of the slings and arrows of life's outrageous fortunes than their brief years on the planet warrant. Some come from families where drug addiction is rampant. Others come from circumstances of extreme poverty. Some have fallen prey to the allure of drugs such as cocaine and crystal meth, others to softer drugs. Some have been bullied. Others just do not fit in. For Joe, it makes no difference. He adopts all of these students as his own.

Second is *respect for others*. Joe's belief, learned through experience and reflection, is that respect for others begins with respect for yourself. He feels that respect is a lot like love: it's difficult to love another person unless you love yourself. Likewise, it's difficult to respect others if you have little or no respect for yourself.

Third is the fostering of *discipline*. In Joe's world, discipline and toughness go hand in hand. Toughness, he stresses to students, lies not in becoming the toughest guy or girl in the school, the goal he aspired to himself as a teenager, but in learning how to face adversity with equanimity and courage. Whether dealing with challenges at school or problems at home, whether standing up to bullying or reaching out to others, discipline consists of overcoming the fears that can paralyze us all and prevent us from doing what's right. Through his own deeds and misdeeds, he's learned that people have a remarkable capacity to go beyond what they think is possible, particularly when they receive the support of others.

Fourth is *self-reflection*. In academic circles, this asset is known as metacognition, the ability to step back and reflect on one's own learning, or lack thereof. Joe spent considerable portions of his life reacting to situations around him, fuelled by values that were often a mirror image of his father's. Sometimes, these served him well. Other times, they got him into trouble, especially when his judgment was altered by alcohol or drugs. His infamous barroom brawl in Kelowna is a prime example of how a simple maxim—"Don't take shit from anyone"—can lead to serious problems when misapplied. Increasingly, Joe has learned to take a deep breath before acting. It took Joe the better part of a lifetime to get there, and he wants to share his experience with others so they can do the same.

Fifth is a *belief in a power greater than oneself*, however you understand this concept. A critical plank in Alcoholics Anonymous and its offshoot programs, Narcotics Anonymous and Gamblers Anonymous, for instance, this asset is sometimes misunderstood as an attempt to inculcate religious beliefs in others. Rather, it is simply an acknowledgement that we are all subject to forces greater than ourselves. No one knows this better than Joe.

Together with academic success and physical well-being, the assets Yo Bro Yo Girl promotes are designed to foster resilience in every student. All of us face adversity at various points in our lives. Being resilient means possessing the confidence, the skills and the perspective to deal with setbacks so that we not only survive them but emerge from the experience stronger.

Research has also shown that the most resilient youth in situations of disadvantage are those who have positive relationships with at least one influential and caring adult. Joe becomes one of those positive, caring adults for these young men and women. He has travelled to the depths of hell and has emerged stronger, kinder and more committed to good as a result of the experience. He's prepared to back his students to whatever extent humanly possible. He also understands that at times he needs to step back and let his students handle things for themselves. True empowerment, he's come to realize, is having the confidence to let his students direct their own lives.

IMAGINE AN AUDITORIUM jammed to the aisles with students aged thirteen to eighteen. There's palpable excitement as they await the arrival of the former Hells Angel who's coming to speak to them for the first time. The stage is illuminated by a single followspot trained on a wooden podium placed precisely in the centre of the stage. A glass of water adorns the podium, the only prop other than a microphone that's visible to the audience.

After a brief introduction by the school principal, Joe emerges from behind the curtain and strides to the podium. He squints into the blackness in front of him until faces slowly begin to emerge. As he runs a hand through his hair, a huge smile settles across his face.

"Great to be here! Time for a story."

With that basic greeting, Joe launches into the story—his story. He begins by telling the students a little about himself.

As you have heard, my name is Joe. I am just another guy, a person like each and every one of you. I grew up in Vancouver's east side, the oldest in a loving family of Italian immigrant parents. My mom and dad worked hard to make sure that we kids had a better life than they did. What immigrant parent does not want a better life for their kids? I have one younger brother and one younger sister. My mother is still alive, but Dad, sadly, passed away a couple of years back—a huge loss in my life and the life of our family.

If you had seen me as a young kid, you would never, ever have thought that this cute little boy would end up with the life he did. You probably would have thought that he would become a model citizen, the kind of person our society—at its best—is built around. You would have been right. But you would also have been wrong, dead wrong. And that's what makes my life story unique and why I am before you today.

My dad was a hardscrabble kind of guy. Some would call him a hard-ass. Tough as nails. When I came home from elementary school one day, bullied and beaten, my dad made me get in the car. We went back to the school, where I was told by him in no uncertain terms to point out the kid who had been bullying me. I thought for sure that Dad was going to get out of the car and beat the crap out of that kid.

Not my dad. He stopped the car right beside the kid in question. But instead of him getting out, he turned to me, looked me straight in the eye and said, "Joe, go over there right now and fight him."

"Are you kidding me, Dad? That kid will kill me."

"Either he will or I will. You are better off with him. Now get going."

With that, I went straightaway to the boy and punched him as hard as I could, right in the nose, before he even realized what was happening. The fight was on.

Luckily, it went okay. I did not get killed. In fact, I probably would have given myself the decision if I were judging it. Whatever, bully-boy never bothered me again. Nor did he bother any of my friends.

You see, from my dad I learned that in life you cannot allow yourself to be pushed around—ever. The lesson I failed *to learn at the time, though, is if you go through life always looking for an opportunity to fight someone, you will never be disappointed. Somebody cuts you off in a car. Time for a fight. Someone pays too much attention to your girlfriend or boyfriend. Time for a fight. Someone is more respected than you are for being tough. Time for a fight. Someone even looks at you the wrong way. Time for a fight. You see, if you go through life looking for fights, you will be permanently employed.*

But where will it get you? I'll tell you where it got me. In high school I didn't care about being the best student I could be or being the best athlete or musician I could be. No, I did not care if I excelled in soccer, a game I loved, or on drums, an instrument that I love to this day. I only cared about being the toughest, most feared badass in the various schools I attended.

Joe steps back for a moment, scanning the audience while he collects his thoughts. The students sit attentively. Not a word is uttered, even by kids who normally chit-chat during assemblies and routinely have to be reprimanded for it.

Joe returns to the microphone. *Various schools? That's right. Various schools! You see, I rarely lasted very long in any of them. Got kicked out of several. Finally landed at Templeton Secondary School in Vancouver's east side, where I graduated. Don't know how that happened, but it did, and I am grateful it did. Probably due in retrospect to some teachers who truly cared for me and had my back.*

Anyway, after that, I went to BCIT and took business courses. Even started my own cell phone company, which became successful, growing in fairly short order to three locations. But still, I was drawn to the dark side of life—fighting, drugs and girls, the more the better. I wanted the respect of others. I thought I got it all right. But remember, being feared is not the same thing as being respected. A few people respected me. They genuinely did. Many more feared me.

After some personal losses—one of my very best friends was killed in a car accident at that point—I made a decision. That's right, a decision, crazy as it seems looking back. I decided I wanted to join a gang, only I didn't call it a gang. I called it a club—a brotherhood. My brotherhood of choice: the Hells Angels. Only problem, membership in the Hells Angels was not easy to come by. I had to earn my way in, which I set about doing.

Now, you might ask why. Why would a guy whose life was on a very good track—his own successful business, girlfriends galore and a family he loved—decide to risk it all to join a gang? Trust me, I have asked myself that question many times over. The best answer I can offer is that it is all part of my journey—all part of a greater purpose in life.

Initially, things were good. Very good. Being a full-patch Nomad, the highest of the high in the Hells Angels, gave me instant and widespread respect. I was part of a family, surrounded by men I respected and loved. That's right, loved. They were a second family to me.

But over time, things began to unravel. I found myself doing more and more drugs, not just of the soft variety but harder stuff: GHB, crack cocaine, that kind of stuff. By now, I had two boys of my own. I became increasingly concerned for their safety. Some might call it paranoia. Whatever the case, I could not leave my house without doing a scan of the neighbourhood to make sure that they—and I—were not in harm's way. I always made sure my gun was tucked into my belt within easy reach.

I was deep into it all right, so deep that I could not see any way out. Not that I really wanted out. That was the funny thing. Drugs do that to you. They totally mess with your head, your ability to think rationally.

Anyway, a couple of other things from this period of my life are worth mentioning. My family—God bless them—stood by me. They knew what I was doing, but they did not turn their backs on me, and for that I am eternally grateful. Another thing is that I was starting to realize that respect and fear are opposite sides of the same coin. I began to question whether I was respected or feared. And if it was the latter, did I really want to live my life in an environment where intimidation was the master and fear the slave?

Gang life is not what you might suppose. It is not all glitz and glamour: big money, fast cars, beautiful women, widespread respect. It is a life where people live in constant alertness if not outright fear, where one single wrong move can result in your death, or the death of someone you love. But don't take my word for it. When you go home this afternoon, just do an Internet search of the words "Gangsters killed in Vancouver area." Trust me, you will see what I mean. It reads like your honour roll. The difference is there is no honour in getting your life cut short by another gangster's bullet. No honour at all.

Two turning points took place in my life. First off, I was arrested for an assault in Kelowna that received widespread media attention, no doubt fuelled by the fact that I was wearing my patch when it happened. All caught on a security camera. Not very smart on my part. Not good for me. Not good for the club.

The second thing that followed was that the club and I had a mutual parting of the ways, due in no small measure to my increasing reliance on crack cocaine and my unpredictability. I ended up bouncing from crack house to crack house. To look at me now, you would not guess that at that stage in my life I was all skin and bone—what you might call the "walking dead."

I ended up being arrested once again, this time for selling a small rock of cocaine, about $10 worth, to an undercover RCMP officer. Thrown into a stark jail cell, all metal bars and concrete floor. So much for the glamorous life of the gangster. I was a wreck, a human tragedy. The only thing I had were the clothes on my back, smelly as they were, and the grit and grime under my fingernails. Not a thing more, not even dignity.

By all rights, I should have been dead. I have known many people who are dead now whose circumstances were a whole lot better than my own. Somehow I survived. My belief is that I survived so that I can share my life story with you and so that you can make wiser decisions than I made. After all, it was not so long ago that I was you—sitting in an auditorium of students, looking to a future that held numerous possibilities, some good, some bad.

While I was in jail, a Vancouver cop by the name of Kevin Torvik showed up. He was not there to question me nor to add to my arrest record. He showed up because he cared. Not to get too deeply into it, but Kevin and I attended high school together. He was younger than me by one year, but he knew me and I him, especially given our more recent history. Kevin served on the Vancouver Police Department's Outlaw Motorcycle Gang Unit, which meant that our paths often crossed—too often for my liking.

But here he was, reaching out to me with a McDonald's bag full of food, one human being to another. We talked for something like three hours, in between my mouthfuls of fries, burgers and chicken fingers, and at some point during that conversation I told Kevin that when I pulled out of the mess I was in, I wanted to work with kids.

You can imagine Kevin's shock and disbelief. "Sure, Joe. Here you are, lying on a concrete floor, looking like hell, a drug addict, a petty criminal—and you want to work with youth. That makes total sense."

He might have said this. He would have been completely within his rights to say to do so. But he did not. The amazing thing is that Kevin, like others in my life, still believed in me. At the very least he—like they—did not indicate otherwise. My *road to recovery has been long and arduous. But here I am, my ambition realized.*

What I have to tell you is this: I have walked with the devil. I have lived and seen stuff that I never, ever want you to see or endure—or for my own children to see or endure. Once gang life gets a hold of you, it is like an eagle clutching its prey with a talon that is relentless, a talon that will squeeze the life out of you slowly, methodically, surely. It has you in its clutch and won't let go.

The thing is, it doesn't matter how tough you are or think you are. The devil known as gang life doesn't care. It takes your pride and chips away at it with cold, uncaring determination. It will seduce you and then strangle you. Even if you are one of the lucky ones who survives—who doesn't join the dishonour roll—you die a kind of slow death anyway. The glamour you sought becomes a living nightmare.

Joe steps back from the podium to take a sip from his glass of water. The students sit quietly, the cavernous auditorium as silent as if it were empty.

You have choices to make. We all have choices to make. And trust me, you will make them, some good, some bad. My only hope is that you will remember what I have shared with you today when facing the most critical of these. Don't be seduced by false promises. Don't be pressured into doing something you know to be wrong. I know this may seem trite, but if something sounds too good to be true, it probably is. Gang life is like that. It is subtle, very subtle, creeping up on you in tiny increments. But like everything else in life, it consists of a series of decisions. I know. I made them. My decision to hang out with certain people. My decision to build my image as a fighter. My decision to do drugs. My decision to carry a gun. Even my decision to honour my friend Naz's commitment to earn the Hells Angels patch.

But we are not going to leave you without support. After today, there will be follow-up. Your teachers and counsellors will work with you to help you plan your journey—where you go from here and how you plan to get there. The organization I represent, the Yo Bro Yo Girl Youth Initiative, will be here to help as well. You will not be alone, just as I was not alone when I lay in that jail cell, a broken man.

Please allow me to leave you with a single thought: I have committed my life to helping you realize there is a better way to find what you are looking for. I ask respectfully, are you prepared to do the same?

Applause fills the auditorium, rising to a crescendo. Joe is visibly moved. He brushes his hand over his hair as if uncertain of what to do next. He smiles: not the cocky smile of the toughest guy in his high school but the smile of someone who does what he does in order to make a difference. No matter how many presentations he gives, no matter how large or small the audience, he still finds it humbling to be where he is at this moment in his life. He never wants that to change.

When the applause dies down, Joe takes questions from the assembled students.

"Did you ever kill anyone?"

"No."

"Did you ever get shot at?"

"Yes."

"Do you still own a motorcycle, and if so what kind?"

"Yes, a Harley-Davidson. A real beauty, if I do say so myself."

Joe draws the Q and A to a close just before the dismissal bell rings. After praising the students for their attention and thanking them for their warm welcome, he acknowledges the staff for their support as well. He closes by letting everyone know that Yo Bro Yo Girl is only a phone call or an email away. Then he makes his exit.

DAK MOLNAR AND JOE reconnected in 2016 through Joe's work with Yo Bro Yo Girl. Dak too has moved on from the heady days of the early 2000s. Today, he's a successful developer, investor and philanthropic community member who's been a major fundraiser with BC Women's Hospital in Vancouver. He's thrown his support behind the work Brenda, Joe and the YBYG team are doing.

Dak describes his old friend today as having the same passion in his eyes as he once did, but with one significant difference.

"Joe has filled his life with all the things he'd left outside it before," he says. "Love. Openness. Kids. A desire to help. You can tell he wants to make a difference for others. There are friends from back in the day who say to me, 'Are you sure? Are you sure that he's changed?' I'm sure. Today, Joe's got all those things you want in a good human being."

15

O N May 8, 2014, the west building of the Vancouver Convention Centre, an architectural
marvel situated on the city's bustling inner
harbour, was home to a special ceremony now in its sixteenth
year: an event known as the Courage to Come Back Awards.
Administered by Coast Mental Health and supported by generous sponsors, the awards celebrate exactly what their name
implies. Each year, six remarkable individuals who have defied
great adversity are recognized. Among the recipients in 2014
was Joe Calendino.

A growing crowd gathered in the massive foyer outside the
centre's ballroom. The night was dark, rain steadily pounding
the spacious patio beyond the glass. The crowd was dressed as
befit the occasion, and four members of the RCMP were there
in their dress reds, a standout in any crowd.

Joe looked impressive in a dark-blue suit newly purchased
for the occasion. Brenda Frisse looked equally striking in a
knee-length black dress and shimmering cream-coloured
jacket. They posed proudly for pictures before entering the ballroom. The event was sold out, and more than twelve hundred

people took their places at the tables that filled the room. There was a palpable buzz as everyone waited for things to start.

To the beat of theme music that could easily have heralded two boxers entering the ring, the emcees for the evening, local media personalities Kevin Evans and Deborra Hope, walked onto the stage. Once they'd outlined the purpose of the evening, talked about the important work Coast Mental Health does and introduced the dignitaries in the audience, Vancouver Chief of Police Jim Chu among them, the award recipients and their stories were presented one by one.

There was Kennedy Baker, a young woman who'd been shot, survived breast cancer surgery at age fifteen and been bullied by classmates but now serves others through a foundation called STAND. Kris Stanbra, from Castlegar, British Columbia, had been flung forty feet from her vehicle in a horrific car crash and told she would never walk again or have children. She willed herself not only to walk but to give birth to two sons, and now she works tirelessly on behalf of people with disabilities. Paul Caune, a middle-aged man who has lived his life with muscular dystrophy, battled through depression to fight the injustices of an uncaring medical system and to create opportunities for others through an organization he heads called Civil Rights Now! Brenda Gardiner, an Indigenous woman who survived sexual assault as a child and witnessed her mother's murder by her father at age eleven, graduated from college to raise her own family and become a respected First Nations leader. Jackie Hooper, an eighty-seven-year-old sparkplug of a woman, had survived an abusive marriage and debilitating depression to earn three degrees and found a supportive housing model for people with mental illness.

And then there was Joe.

His story, like the others, unfolded on a series of massive screens placed strategically around the room. There was young

Joe, fresh-faced and innocent-looking, described in earnest tones as a "fighter" at age fourteen. There was Joe the businessman, standing proudly outside one of his stores. There was an image of Joe in menacing sunglasses as the narrator described his decision to enter a gang. There was Joe the gangster, in grainy black and white on the security tape, pounding and kicking a male much larger than himself in the crowded Kelowna casino, his Hells Angels patch clearly visible. Finally, there was Joe the ex-Angel, shown with some of the young people whose lives he has so positively affected.

After the video ended, Joe crossed to the podium, drew a pair of reading glasses from his jacket pocket and unfolded his script.

"I was great until I got on the stage," he began. "Now I'm nervous. I would like to thank Coast Mental Health for the honour of receiving this prestigious award. I would also like to congratulate my fellow recipients and tell you what a privilege it is to share this award with you.

"When Lorne Segal, chair of the BC campaign, phoned and told me I was the recipient of a Courage to Come Back Award for 2014, I took a deep breath and wiped the tears from my eyes. This time, they were tears of joy. So many things were racing through my head. I remember all the other tears I have shed— tears of fear, tears of pain, for myself and for all the others I have hurt along the way: my family, my friends and so many others.

"Fighting and beating addiction takes a team effort. Without others believing in me, I wouldn't be standing here today. I'd have given up. Addiction knows no bounds. It plays cruel tricks on how you think. I thought I'd lose everything: my family, my friends, the will to live. It was through the strength and support of these very people, including those I once thought of as my enemies, that I was able to find the courage to come back. Through their belief in me, I began to believe in myself.

"Trying to live healthy was one thing. Trying to figure out what to do with the rest of my life—that was a big thing. All I

YBYG participants celebrate their 2nd place finish at the provincial BJJ tournament.

Wrapping up summer school with teacher Fran Alley's students. In addition to Fran (far right), the other adults are Brenda Calendino, far left, and Gary Little, second from right.

Joe with Superintendent Jordan Tinny of the Surrey school district (to Joe's left); John Wilson of the RCMP (to Joe's right); and Rob Rai (far right) of Surrey Safe Schools, along with YBYG youth.

Joe addresses over a thousand guests as he accepts one of the 2014 Courage to Come Back awards.

Joe's four sons were the connection that helped him survive his darkest days. Son Jo Jo, his eldest, born January 12, 2002.

Second-eldest son Matteo, born January 9, 2005.

Luca, born September 15, 2006.

Domenic, born October 27, 2007.

Joe's four boys enjoying time with three of Brenda's grandchildren.

A meeting with Governor General David Johnston and Sharon Johnston with, from left to right, Fran Alley, Kevin Torvik and Brandon Steele.

Theresa Campbell and Toby Hinton, long-standing supporters of Joe and YBYG.

Following a challenging martial arts workout with pizza at a nearby Commercial Drive outlet.

From left to right, Kevin Torvik, Andy Amoroso and Rob Cortese join Joe, their lifelong friend, for a special photo.

Brenda's family celebrates the wedding of their mother/grandmother.

Brandon Steele, Brenda and Joe. The "cop I most hated" is now a close friend and co-presenter.

A delighted Nerina with her new daughter-in-law.

Nerina with Joe at Federico's nightclub, site of Joe and Brenda's wedding reception.

Eva, with brother Ralph alongside, takes the microphone at Joe and Brenda's wedding. Eva noted, "I never thought the next speech I would give on Joe's behalf would be at his wedding. Never."

Brenda and Joe enjoy a brief period of quiet at their not-so-quiet wedding.

Amanda Tabert and Willy DuGray, YBYG mentors
extraordinaire.

knew was that I needed to make it right. I needed to give back. It seemed like a lifetime ago I had coached kids in soccer. As I was lying on that jail-cell floor, I realized that I wanted to do whatever it took to prevent kids from going down the same path.

"When I first mentioned this to the officer who was kind enough to see past the addiction, past the ex-gangster to the man who lay broken on the floor, he handed me a bag of McDonald's. Kevin, I no longer eat McDonald's," Joe said, nodding in Kevin Torvik's direction. The audience laughed. Joe waited for the noise to die down before continuing.

"'Get yourself clean and sober,' Kevin said, 'and I will do everything to make it happen.'

"And so, with the support of my family, I got clean, and he delivered. He connected me with a number of officers, a lot of officers, school district people—I am engaged to marry one—and it's there my story begins. I was able to get my foot in the door and start working with kids. It's real simple for me. You don't have to stop something you haven't started. It's the best way to sum up the message I try to send whenever given the opportunity."

Joe talked a bit more. About how he met Brenda, and the extended family they share. About the strength he has received from his family, friends and the organizations that have supported him in his recovery. About the work he now does with youth and his partners, in the school system and elsewhere.

Finally, he said, "This one's tough." He paused. The pause got longer and longer. He struggled with the words on the script in front of him, trying to compose himself before uttering them. "This one's for you, Dad."

The music that heralded Joe's exit from the stage was nearly drowned out by the applause.

Some time later, after everyone had spoken, money for Coast Mental Health had been raised, and Joe Segal, a local businessman and revered philanthropist, had been honoured for his support of the awards, Joe's son Lorne took to the podium to offer the evening's closing remarks.

"When I phoned Joe Calendino to tell him he had won a Courage to Come Back Award," Lorne told the audience, "I could hear him cry. As he composed himself, Joe said to me, 'You know, I'm not supposed to be here. I'm looking out the window right now to the mountain that lies beyond. When we hang up, Lorne, I know I will have to climb it.'"

16

COMMERCIAL Drive on Vancouver's east side has a rich history. It began as a skid road, constructed according to the technology of the day—narrow-diameter logs laid crosswise and loosely covered with sand to create an intricate system of roller bearings. Logs were transported along these roads in all kinds of weather, though skid roads often played havoc with the hoofs of horses. Shifts in the structure created gaps between the logs, through which horses' legs could drop precipitously, often leading to tragic outcomes.

From the Drive's hardscrabble beginnings, the area evolved into a neighbourhood reflecting Vancouver's multicultural mosaic. Immigrants poured into the area, originally from Italy, Portugal and China, more recently from Africa, India and Latin America. Public housing abounds in the neighbourhood and is contiguous with houses that fetch well over a million dollars today in Vancouver's stratospheric real estate market.

The area is also home to a vibrant counterculture. The Vancouver Dyke March takes place on the Drive every year, as did the now-defunct Day of the Dead–themed Parade of Lost Souls, along with an annual jam-packed celebration called Italian Day. Every four years, during the global spectacle that is FIFA's World Cup of soccer, the Drive comes alive in an even more electric way. Fans from the winning countries drive up and down the street, car horns honking incessantly, the flags of their home countries flapping wildly from windows and makeshift staffs.

It was in this neighbourhood that Joe and Brenda decided to celebrate a very important event in their lives. On June 29, 2014, they were married at Federico's Supper Club, a long-standing institution on Commercial Drive.

The day started out as so many do in Vancouver. Rain poured down on the city and its environs, occasional rays of sunshine breaking through the cloud cover. By the time guests began arriving at Federico's in the late afternoon, to the accompaniment of exuberant soccer fans celebrating the latest World Cup winner—tiny Costa Rica, as it turned out—the sun was bathing the scene in brilliant light.

In the club's dim interior, guests huddled in small groups, reconnecting and making new acquaintances. Joe's sister, Eva, rushed about, welcoming everyone and making sure they had seats at one of the several tables grouped around the dance floor. Joe's mom, Nerina, looked radiant, her shimmering black-and-white top complementing an understated pair of black pants and open-toed shoes. Joe's brother, Ralph, played the role of family ambassador, greeting guests with the charm and grace of a skilled maître d'. Joe's four boys dashed about the empty dance floor with the energy only those approaching their teen years can muster.

Brenda's family—daughters Val, Kirby and Jessica, and son, Jake—was there in full force as well, looking like they had just stepped out of a fashion layout. Their spouses and partners joined them at a large table close to the edge of the dance floor, along with Brenda's five grandchildren.

The other guests formed an eclectic mix. At one table sat several police officers, including Kevin Torvik, Brandon Steele and Doug Spencer. At another table sat members of the Yo Bro Yo Girl Board, Nick Bedford, Andrew Schofield, Bill Burd and Gary Little among them. Seated here and there were other notables: Yo Bro Yo Girl student mentors Willy, Teresa, Amanda and Jovan; Rob Cortese and Andy Amoroso, lifelong friends of Joe's, along with their wives, Toni and Linda; and Joe's judo partners Mark Steinkamp, Al Arsenault and Brian Shipper.

At 5:30 p.m., the wedding commissioner summoned Brenda and Joe to a spot near the club's small stage. With a smile on her face, the commissioner had Brenda and Joe repeat their vows. When Ralph stepped forward with the rings, the commissioner directed Joe and Brenda to place them on each other's fingers.

There was a moment of mild confusion when Joe extended his right hand to accept his ring. The amused wedding commissioner noted the error and corrected it. Joe extended his left hand, and Brenda slipped a gold band with tiny diamond chips onto his ring finger. Joe's dad, Frank, would have been proud beyond words. His eldest son had not only married a wonderful woman; he now wore the ring Frank himself had worn throughout his marriage to Nerina. The formal ceremony complete, the audience erupted in spontaneous applause.

From there, the staff of Federico's wheeled into action, taking orders from the guests and ensuring that the evening would be as pleasurable for them as it would be for Joe and Brenda.

Dinner was marked by lots of clinking of cutlery on glasses and coffee cups, signalling to Joe and Brenda that it was time for a kiss. This was an Italian wedding, after all. The speeches that followed were brief, heartfelt and few in number. When it was Joe's turn to say a few words, he was characteristically succinct and sincere. "I know Dad is with us right now," he said, a swell of emotion briefly overcoming him, before acknowledging the coming together of two families and two life journeys. Brenda stood at his side, letting Joe speak for the two of them. Cameras appeared from every pocket and purse.

The first few bars of John Legend's "All of Me" burst from the club's sound system: time for the first waltz. Joe and Brenda, alone on the dance floor, held each other close. The cameras continued to click, amateur photographers doing their own two-steps as they tried to capture the best angle possible.

The inaugural dance complete, Joe's cousin Federico Fuoco made his way to the stage. He took his place behind a bank of keyboards and computers, as he had done thousands of times before, treating the crowd to an inimitable mix of songs old and new. The guests danced with gusto.

The guests filed out in small groups of three and four as midnight approached. The air was clear and invigorating, a far cry from the heavy dampness of the morning rain. As Joe exited Federico's, he looked skyward. The contrast between what his life had been and what it had become could not have been more pronounced. In that instant, in that time and place, he knew he was the luckiest man on the planet.

17

BRITANNIA Elementary School is in the neighbourhood where Brenda Frisse grew up, a part of the city not far from where Joe spent the majority of his youth. Justin Borsato teaches Grade 7 there. Honoured in 2012 as the first recipient of the University of British Columbia's Alumni Teacher Award for extraordinary teaching, Borsato exhibits an obvious love of his students and possesses tireless energy. Mr. B., as the students call him, is acutely aware that the decisions students make at this stage of their lives affect what follows—thus his decision to engage the services of Joe Calendino.

Borsato is enthusiastic in describing Joe's work with students. "Joe Calendino," he says, "has armed my students with the tools to avoid the devastating pitfalls surrounding drugs, alcohol and gangs. His lessons have cut to the core of the issues plaguing at-risk and inner-city students. Because of Joe's contributions to my classroom, these students have not only the tools but also the confidence to use them."

On an afternoon during the 2014–15 school year, Joe, wearing a black track suit with the Yo Bro Yo Girl insignia emblazoned on it, enters Borsato's classroom to a warm welcome from the students seated in groups at their various tables. Joe acknowledges the salutations as he heads to the front of the class to connect his antiquated Mac notebook to the projector. He's planning to show them *No Ordinary Joe*, a PowerPoint presentation that borrows its title from the Odd Squad production featuring photos gathered from Joe's life, as well as video clips, many of them excerpted from local news coverage. The montage has a kind of reverse flow to it. We see a young man whose high level of fitness is obvious to the viewer—a boxer, fists raised, posing for the camera like a young Rocky Marciano or Tony Galento. We see Joe standing alongside his motorcycle, Marlon Brando style, and then in full patch, his ascendancy to the peak of the biker world complete.

The presentation shifts abruptly to show Joe the cocaine addict, a stringy-haired, vacant-eyed individual the students barely recognize. Joe hits the pause button on the presentation and addresses the class.

"Let me tell you, addiction knows no boundaries. Mental health issues know no boundaries. Trust me; I have stared both of them in the face. So how does all this start? When does it start? I want to share information with you, not to 'scare you straight.' That's not what we are about—furthermore, it doesn't work—but to give you an idea of what addiction might look like in your lives should you ever make the choice to start."

The kids Joe is addressing are no more than twelve years old, but some of them have already seen and experienced more than many people will in a lifetime. Joe knows this. He knows that these students must be reached now; tomorrow, for many, will be too late.

On the screen, a young Indigenous woman stares into the camera. She discusses the recruitment of young women, often Indigenous, into Alberta street gangs.

"We like them big and young—the bigger the better," she says. Her credo and that of her gang is simple: "If the targets opt not to join the gang, they are harassed, followed on the streets, regularly and viciously beaten up."

The point is not lost on Mr. B.'s students, many of whom are Indigenous themselves. "You see," Joe emphasizes, "it's not just boys who have to be aware of gang recruitment. It's also you girls. You need to ensure that you do not put yourselves into situations or surround yourselves with 'friends' that lead to gang membership. You need to develop skills to go along with an attitude that says, 'Not me. I have a better plan for my life than that.' My commitment to you is this: I will help you develop these skills as we make this journey together."

Staying with the theme of gender in the gang world, Joe asks the students how young women who "hang with" gangsters are portrayed. His question follows a particularly unsettling part of the PowerPoint presentation in which young women—girlfriends and associates of well-known local gangsters—are featured. One is dead, her dazzling smile a thing of the past. Another is paralyzed after being filled with bullets intended for her gangster boyfriend; her life has been irrevocably changed, many would say ruined. Others have gone missing and are presumed dead.

The students are quiet, thinking about Joe's question. A boy finally breaks the silence. "They're toys," he says, "nothing but toys."

Joe nods. He talks about the risks incurred by those associating with gang members, from the girlfriend "toys" to a stereo installer—not a gang member himself—who was gunned down while driving a gangster's chrome-laden Escalade to the shop to install a new sound system. "Wrong place. Wrong time. No more. No less."

"You see," Joe concludes, "there are several elements at play here, any one of which can lead to the senseless tragedies we have seen in these videos. Before you ever, ever make a decision to become part of a gang, let me leave you with one last clip."

The screen springs to life once again, revealing a man in his mid-twenties who talks about his entry into a Vancouver gang. "I want out," he says matter-of-factly, "but I can't get out. I'm locked in. You see, I have made too many enemies. There is nowhere I can go to get away. Absolutely nowhere."

When he is asked by the interviewer to predict his future, the young man's voice takes on a kind of weariness, a resignation that comes from knowing all too well what end is in store for him. That end came soon. His interview is followed by a news report showing a vehicle into which multiple shots have been fired, broken glass all that remains of the various entry points. Police tape and traffic cones envelop the young man's car, the focal point of an official crime scene. He has been executed. The Grade 7 students sit silent.

In the last few minutes of the class, some of the students accept Joe's challenge to join a mock gang that will oppose Joe's mock gang in their next get-together. What Joe wants to show them is just how easy it is to get locked into these kinds of groups—and, as in the case of the young man in the PowerPoint presentation, how difficult it is to get out. Joe's theme, and his challenge, is to show students that there is a better way and to help ensure they have the skills, the assets, necessary to create viable lifelong options.

The bell sounds. The school day has ended, but not for Joe. After chatting with some of the students, he heads to a room in the school's basement that can best be described as utilitarian. It abuts storage areas where tumbling mats are piled high, mats that will be used for the martial arts training Joe provides to his Yo Bro Yo Girl mentors.

AS AN ORGANIZATION like YBYG matures, people who have benefited from its support often seek ways to give back. One way to do that is through volunteering. Another is through donating money. In the case of Yo Bro Yo Girl, an important way to stay involved is through peer mentoring.

High school students who have participated in Yo Bro Yo Girl and maintained a successful commitment to it are asked if they're interested in mentoring younger students. If the answer is yes—which it usually is—they then receive some training. These aspiring mentors are coached in such skills as active listening and group facilitation. They learn how to help others problem-solve without imposing solutions of their own. They share their own stories with their mentees, not to one-up the younger students but to help them see potential solutions in the experience of others.

Once they've completed the training, the peer mentors are assigned to groups of younger students, typically those who are about to enter high school and so are at their most vulnerable. Having a caring older student support them through this transition is key. Participating in the Yo Bro Yo Girl after-school program can mean the "at risk" label is soon jettisoned in favour of "at school and succeeding."

JOE LOOKS AT his watch. It's well past 3:30 p.m., the appointed start time for the Yo Bro Yo Girl group. He is puzzled. What's going on? Not a single member of the group has shown up.

"Totally uncharacteristic," says Joe to a guest who has come to observe the session." I think they might have their grad photos today. Yeah, I guess that's why no one is here."

A few more minutes elapse. Finally, a student opens the door. He pokes his head in tentatively, then, seeing Joe, breaks into a huge smile. "You *are* here. We're upstairs in the community centre today."

"I'll be right there," Joe tells the young man.

"That's what I love about these kids," Joe says on the way upstairs. "Just when I think they have something else on the go, they always come through. They wouldn't miss their Yo Bro Yo Girl meetings for the world."

Nine students are waiting for Joe. He banters with each of them. Dressed in the loose-fitting gi worn by martial artists, he's every bit the Kung Fu sensei addressing his followers. But Joe doesn't consider these students to be his pupils. In his mind, they are his equals. There's a saying in Yo Bro Yo Girl: "Leave your ego on the mat." That applies to mentor and mentee alike. Just as they learn from him, he learns from them.

"Let's take a few minutes to work on our breathing, to meditate," Joe begins. "Focus on the flow of your breathing. In, out. In, out. Good. Now, you remember what we did here last time. We talked about self-defence. I demonstrated what to do in certain situations. Let's review."

He points to a girl with a slight build and summons her to the front. With her back to Joe, facing the other members of the group, she sits on the mat with her legs folded beneath her.

Joe role-plays the attacker.

"Now, what if I come up behind Tammy and grab her by the throat?" He demonstrates what this might look like in real life. "Right away, you notice that she does something that is not necessarily instinctive but is something that we've learned. She draws her chin as close to her chest as possible, so that the attacker can't choke her."

Joe asks the young woman to relax her position so he can show the class what typically happens in an attack of this type and how to defend themselves against it. The class sits rapt.

"It's important that girls learn to be assertive, confident," Joe tells them. "Girls, you cannot live in fear. You should not and do not have to live in fear. Learning how to protect yourself, while not a cure-all, certainly helps. And while I'm at it, boys, never forget that when a girl says no, she means no. End of story. Full stop. Be respectful. Always."

Joe thanks Tammy and then points to Nam, a wiry young man who earlier had been entertaining others in the group with a random display of flexibility and speed, his hands working in tandem as he punched the protective padding fixed to the concrete wall. He exudes confidence and joie de vivre.

"Nam, sit down here."

Nam assumes the same position Tammy took earlier, positioning himself directly in front of Joe.

Joe addresses the group. "The difference between the hold I'm about to show you and others we have seen so far is this: with your forearm or leg or shoulder, you can end up breaking the attacker's bone—or bones. Four to six weeks later, maybe eight weeks, they are back in business, the cast removed. Serious, but not too serious. You have protected yourself. With this hold, though, the chokehold or sleeper hold—call it what you will—you can actually kill someone."

Joe puts his right arm underneath Nam's chin, tightening the hold ever so slightly. Nam winces. He's clearly uncomfortable, though his smile remains. Joe demonstrates how to leverage the hold. Slowly, Nam's smile disappears.

"With a sharp torque of this arm, you can literally break the person's neck," Joe says. He applies a little more pressure before releasing the hold. Nam shakes his head as a dog might shake water from its coat.

"You okay?" Joe asks.

"Fine," Nam responds, though the continued rolling of his neck back and forth seems to indicate otherwise. His smile returns slowly.

Joe concludes by stressing that self-defence should never be the first point of defence. Typically, it is the last. Avoidance and evasion are the best options to avert trouble. If and when these fail, however, it's important for students to have a plan B. That helps build their confidence.

WILLY DUGRAY, AN eighteen-year-old graduate of the Yo Bro program, now works with YBYG as a peer mentor. Wiry of build, five feet nine inches in height, with short-cropped brown hair and brown eyes, Willy sports a black baseball cap adorned with death-metal script. He is articulate, measuring each word, and confident in his presentation. He isn't and has never been a gangster, but he could well have been.

Growing up on the east side of Vancouver, where he attended Sir Wilfred Grenfell Elementary, followed by a short stint at Maywood Community School in Burnaby, Willy knows the harsh realities of life first-hand. His older brother, Dustin, has been in and out of jail, or some form of removal from the family, since Dustin was eight years old. He's now in his mid-twenties. Willy knew that a mere decision or two is all that separates the freedom he enjoys from his brother's life of incarceration.

One of Willy's first decisions upon entering his teen years was to transfer into the alternative education stream of the Vancouver school system. He ended up in a program called Streetfront Alternative, which is committed to helping students build inner strength and interpersonal skills as well as supporting them academically. Led by a creative, high-energy teacher named Trevor Stokes, the program infuses large doses of physical education into the curriculum.

Students in Streetfront are challenged to do what for many of them would have once seemed impossible. They run marathons together. They have planned and made two expeditions to the peak of Mount Kilimanjaro, projects that were as much about team building and realizing their potential as they were about standing atop the mountain for a group photo.

It was through Streetfront that Willy met Joe Calendino. Joe had been invited to speak to the students about Yo Bro Yo Girl and the possibilities it held for them. Willy was struck by Joe's passion, and what really caught his attention—in addition to

Joe's compelling personal narrative—was the fact that Yo Bro Yo Girl was similar to the Streetfront program. It had a vitally important physical component—martial arts—to go along with its focus on personal decision making and healthy living.

Willy was sold. He wanted to learn how to protect himself if it should ever come to that, but even more importantly, he wanted to develop the self-confidence and discipline that martial arts engender.

"When I first came into Grade 8, I was harsh shy," Willy says. "I would never talk to anyone. I had social anxiety problems, so I figured if I got into Yo Bro Yo Girl, with its small classes, I could branch out—develop self-confidence. When I first entered Grade 8, if I wasn't good at something, I wouldn't do it. If I could not dribble a soccer ball better than most others on the team, for example, I wouldn't play soccer. In Yo Bro Yo Girl, you do a lot of work one on one in order to build skills on a foundation of success. That appealed to me. You develop confidence that way."

Ninety percent of success, it is said, is simply showing up. Willy was wise enough even in his early teen years to have figured this out. He looked for a school experience that gave him a reason to be there. He found it in Streetfront. He looked for new opportunities to build on that commitment. These he found in Yo Bro Yo Girl.

"I figured that if I could make a commitment to show up after school for Yo Bro Yo Girl, then that would be a good habit. Even if I got a job later on, I figured that I would be able to combine it and Yo Bro Yo Girl. Looking back, I've tried to give to the program as well as take from it. I have probably volunteered four solid twenty-four-hour days all told, everything from participating in the Odd Squad gala [a fundraiser for the organization] to On Track, a nine-hour experience where we talk about peer-to-peer mentoring and various other things as we walk through Vancouver's Downtown Eastside."

Willy has gained prowess in martial arts and this, he says, is what connects him to other students in the program, an important component of his role as a peer mentor.

"One thing I like about Yo Bro Yo Girl is that so many different people come. Many of them I would not ordinarily talk to, but when they see me and my martial arts ability, they know what I'm talking about and they respect me instantly. I'm able to make connections with them through this, even if we do not like the same music or same dancing or whatever. They show me respect and I always, always show it back. I like when you get to learn with someone you don't ordinarily connect with."

As a peer mentor, Willy serves as a guide to the student population of which he was so recently a member. This, he asserts proudly, is the main way in which the program will grow.

"The same kids who sit in class and just throw out random comments—more like jokes that they try to get a laugh from—will listen to you when you show them something they want to learn. Even kids who have ADHD, and I've worked with a couple who've been diagnosed as such, will listen to your every word when you show them one thing and keep repeating it until they get it. They will get involved. They will not try to shut it out and sit in the corner tossing out random comments. If you push them hard enough and they are somewhat interested, they will get into it. That's what I like."

Willy enumerates some of the successes he has enjoyed as a mentor: three friends who have connected to Yo Bro Yo Girl and benefited from it, along with two fellow students from Streetfront who have done the same and followed through on their commitment to quit smoking pot. Willy follows up with these students to check on their progress and to ensure they'll be coming to the next meeting of the group. He knows his inquiries show others that he cares. He's doing for them what Joe has done for him—providing certainty and support in a world that can be wildly unpredictable and ruthless in its indifference.

Willy's regard for Joe Calendino can be summed up in one word: respect. Words like "intensity" and "dedication" punctuate the conversation. So do anecdotes about how Joe will drop whatever he's doing to go to the aid of a young man or woman who needs his help. "Even if he is overloaded—his plate is full beyond full—he will get it done," Willy says.

The point Willy keeps stressing is that Joe offers opportunity. He respects the right of each individual to buy into the Yo Bro Yo Girl program and its attendant philosophy or not. You either make the commitment to improve your life or you don't. If you do, kudos. If you don't, that's okay, as long as you remember that a decision to exit Yo Bro Yo Girl at this point in your life is not binding. You can always come back, provided you're ready to make a commitment to a better way of life.

"There are always one or two who are not really into it," Willy explains, "but they have three of their friends there who say, 'Come on, man, you have got to do it.' It's not so much peer pressure as accepting the challenge: If your friends can do it, why can't you? The influence of your friends serves as a great motivator."

From the beginning, Yo Bro Yo Girl served as a positive force in Willy's life. He looked at what the program had done for others—school success, job placements, and so on—and knew that was what he wanted for himself. "I wanted to be successful. I didn't want to sit around and smoke weed all day. Who cares what others think? I had no problem working part-time at McDonald's—whatever it took to put money in my pocket and food on the table. Today, thanks to Yo Bro Yo Girl and the people who support it, I work for Global Transport, having earned my Class 1, 3 and 5 driver's licences."

Willy's older brother remains incarcerated, but Willy also knows his brother as a talented artist and poet. The elder

DuGray created a beautiful stained-glass art piece for Joe that reads "Yo Bro" in large letters, as well as crafting a small Harley-Davidson motorcycle for him. The gifts underline his appreciation for the care Joe has given Willy. Dustin DuGray knows where bad decisions lead, and he's grateful that Joe is making a difference for his younger brother and for other young men and women at a critical juncture in their lives. Perhaps Willy's brother would still be a free man, a contributing member of society, had there been a Joe Calendino for him at the same stage of development.

Willy's older sister, Kitty, appreciates what Yo Bro Yo Girl has done for him as well. She's had to deal with her own struggles, including a brain injury suffered when she jumped from the balcony of the family's fourth-floor apartment while she was high. The fact that she's alive is nothing short of miraculous, Willy says. "She's been dealing with things so well, considering there's a dent about this deep right here"—Willy shows with his fingers the depth of the injury—"in her skull."

Willy knows intimately the challenges his brother and sister have endured, and he's doing his level best to ensure that his life is different. He finds fulfillment in his role as a peer mentor, though he's realistic about what he's able to offer. "If somebody comes to me," he says, "and is semi-dependable, I certainly will give them a chance. If they are prepared to show up for the next few sessions of Yo Bro Yo Girl, I can start doing more for them. If, however, they are not prepared to put anything in, then there's nothing I can do for them. There's no point them being there."

Also, Willy says, if someone's reason for joining Yo Bro Yo Girl is to learn some martial arts tricks they can use on a Friday or Saturday night to beat up others, that will not happen on his watch. Yo Bro Yo Girl is all about self-improvement and gaining confidence. Used for these ends, the martial arts component of the program is critically important. Used for any other purpose—the breaking of an arm or the intentional damaging of a tendon—it has no place. Students in Yo Bro Yo Girl understand this and respect it.

On the topic of drug use, Willy is more flexible. He understands that Yo Bro Yo Girl can be a first step in a young person's attempt to break a drug habit and develop a healthier, more positive lifestyle. Furthermore, given the target audience of the program, it's inevitable that many young men and women who could benefit from it are involved to some degree with drug use. Willy, like Joe, wants to give these students a chance. He believes that through positive role modelling and positive experiences in the program, they will be more likely to commit to a drug-free life.

"You can't merely give them an ultimatum," he elaborates. "They don't want that. You have to bring them in and gradually show them that they can be just like us, the people they look up to. 'Look, you can do all of this if you want—just like we do. Is that something you might be interested in? Then we can help you.' You have to ease them into the program and show them why they might want it."

Willy closes the conversation by describing a young man who came to Yo Bro Yo Girl looking to improve his life. Like many young people, though, this individual was conflicted. He couldn't imagine giving up his habit of smoking weed for something that was not yet even partially defined in his mind. He felt his life had little meaning, and weed, if nothing else, helped ease the monotony for him, the pain.

"Why would you come here?" Willy asked the young man. "Because you love what you're doing by being involved in the program. So you find something good and you hold on to that. You do what you love. What better purpose in life is there?"

By asking these questions, Willy guided the way to some critical answers. A young man he describes as being at the crossroads of life was able to make a decision that will enrich his life, perhaps forever.

AMANDA TABERT IS another energetic and articulate senior mentor whose insights into her Yo Bro Yo Girl experience are revealing. She is slight in stature, but her flamboyant hair colour (highlighter pink—though she calls it red) ensures that she will never be lost in a crowd. Standing out in that way is something she would have avoided at all costs at an earlier stage in her life.

Born in Taiwan and raised there until she was eleven, Amanda emigrated to Canada to live with her dad. An introverted youngster, she was initially homeschooled. Eventually, she followed her older sister to City Central Learning Centre, an alternative school in Surrey. Looking back on those days, Amanda notes she not only worked on overcoming her shyness but also supported herself and contributed to her family financially, out of necessity. "I guess what was unusual in some settings—supporting yourself—was pretty normal in my school," she says. "Most kids had to work to supplement family income. For us, school did not come first; it came second."

Along with her classmates, Amanda was exposed to Yo Bro Yo Girl through an engaging presenter named Joe Calendino. "After my sister did Yo Bro Yo Girl with Joe and I followed her to City Central Learning Centre, I remember going up to Joe after he did a presentation for us and asking him, 'When is an after-school program just for girls going to start?' He said he didn't know." Joe and Brenda created Empowering Young Women as a direct response to the increasingly passionate chorus of voices like Amanda's.

The program has a martial arts focus, but in Amanda's words, "that really is a minor part of the program." She soon realized that while the focus was ostensibly on self-defence, the bigger lessons for her and other participants were how to develop self-confidence and resilience.

Amanda refers to a video that was shot early in the program as she and other young women were first mastering the rudiments of martial arts. "I look so timid and so fragile, not at all the way I am now. On the video, I looked like a perfect target. What changed about me was first learning not to look so helpless—more importantly, not to feel so helpless—something I gained through the program."

Amanda's role as a Yo Bro Yo Girl mentor allows her to make a difference for other young women, as well as to continue developing her own sense of self.

"Some of the girls come and go," Amanda says, "but those who stay get so much from the program—and add so much. It's great to see them hold their own on the mats with the boys. This encourages me to do better as well."

Empowering Young Women has become a central part of Yo Bro Yo Girl's offerings. Amanda is adamant that any gender bias that might once have existed in Yo Bro Yo Girl is long gone. She presents an interesting perspective when it comes to the future of YBYG. "It's a scary thought to envision the day where we do this program without Joe, but he wants to ensure all senior mentors are trained and possess the skills and confidence necessary to carry the program by themselves. When he's no longer able to do it or chooses to retire, the program will still flourish. It won't be about Joe. That's really what all of us are working toward."

In addition to gaining prowess in defence-based martial arts, Yo Bro Yo Girl senior mentors earn certificates from the National Coaching Certification Program (NCCP—Level I), as well as cardiopulmonary resuscitation (CPR) certification. They also work with Brenda on fundamental counselling skills: active listening, suicide and violence prevention, and appropriate delegation to the plethora of agencies designed to support young people. With all of this, they acquire a skill set that will help others in the short term and enrich their own lives and the lives of their mentees over the long term.

"If, for example, a kid in your group comes to you with information about something bad happening at home, you know what questions to ask and how best to refer him or her to the appropriate person or agency," Amanda explains. "This type of training is essential so that we don't make mistakes."

When it comes to helping students develop goal-setting strategies, Amanda is clear on her approach. "I don't ever get too personal," she says. "I don't want to come off as preachy or thrust myself into their lives and tell them what to do. For this reason, I listen without judgment and let them direct the conversation."

Amanda is currently studying cognitive psychology at Kwantlen Polytechnic University, one of the courses leading to a degree in psychology. She wants to develop a practice of her own, specializing in forensic psychology. "My long-term goal, within the next twenty years at the very most, is to earn my PhD as well," she says. "It's something that I want to do. It will happen."

Regarding the founders of Yo Bro Yo Girl, Amanda is unequivocal. "I can't thank Joe and Brenda enough for what they have meant to me. They really are special people."

18

KWANTLEN Polytechnic University, January 2016. They present as an odd couple. To the left is the ex-gangster, his hair fashionably long, his dress shirt open at the collar. To the right is the cop, wearing his uniform and sporting closely cropped hair. Even from the back of Kieron McConnell's criminology classroom, the insignia adorning the police officer's uniform is visible on his shoulder: "Police Vancouver" the crest reads. A Canadian flag lies below these words, along with the Latin inscription *Servamus*—"We serve."

Joe Calendino and Brandon Steele are ready to address the expectant audience. The instructor, Kieron McConnell, is a former cop himself. He and Brandon served together on the Gang Crime Unit of the VPD's Organized Crime section. Thirty-two students are there to hear them, roughly half of them female. Many ethnic groups are represented, reflecting the multicultural fabric of the community in which Kwantlen is located.

The police officer begins. "Good morning. My name is Brandon Steele. I am a seventeen-year member with the Vancouver Police Department. I have done patrol. I have worked on the

Pickton investigation and on gang crime, and I am now in the Youth Services section, where I have assumed the newly created portfolio of working exclusively with twenty-three alternative schools in Vancouver that meet a variety of needs for students who do not fit into mainstream high schools.

"To my right is Mr. Joe Calendino. Together, over a number of years, we have created a not-for-profit initiative known as Yo Bro Yo Girl, where we directly work with at-risk youth, primarily in Vancouver and Surrey. What we'd like to do now is share with you a brief video that underscores why we do what we do. The conclusion you'll come to, as we did, is that there is a need for the type of services Yo Bro Yo Girl provides."

With that, Steele steps forward and taps the "on" button of the LED projector. Images gleaned from local newscasts begin flashing across the screen.

The voice of a female broadcaster: "There has been another targeted shooting in Surrey, the fifth since Monday evening." Empty shell casings and yellow police tape mark the scene. That image is followed by documentary-style footage accompanied by a voiceover: "At the end of the 2000s, the gangs running Vancouver faced a reckoning. With most of their bosses either in prison, dead or retired, a new generation of South Asian gang-bangers now dominates the city's thriving cocaine business. But there is a new player on the block, the Somalis, and they are demanding a piece of the action." Carnage fills the screen, the closing image that of a twenty-eight-year-old man "known to police," who has been shot in the leg.

The classroom is quiet. Not a sound can be heard other than Steele reaching down to silence the projector. "That's the backdrop to where we are today," he says, "and where we were five years ago. These things tend to run in cycles, fuelled by drugs, violence and competition for control. The cycles just seem to continue.

"So a group of us saw this need to figure out how we got here and how can we break the cycle. We knew that somebody, some group, has to come along, take control and say, 'We are not going to let the youth of our community go down that path.' Joe and I thus formed an unlikely alliance. We wanted to work with youth who were not yet involved in gang activity but were starting to get involved in activities that could very well lead there.

"Now, one of the interesting phenomena regarding the formation of gangs is that they often arise from informal friend-ships—friendships formed as early as elementary school, in youth community groups and even through seemingly innocent interactions in neighbourhoods. These kids are not recruited by the Red Scorpions or the UN, two of the more infamous gangs in this area. They can simply be groups of guys who grew up together, played street hockey or basketball together, and now do crime together."

Steele expands a little on why today's gang members get drawn into the lifestyle. Glory. Respect. Money. Girls. Exactly the factors that drew Joe Calendino to the lifestyle he chose for himself in his early twenties. Then it is Joe's turn to speak.

"My name is Joe Calendino, and I am the executive director of the Yo Bro Yo Girl Youth Initiative." Joe no longer introduces himself as a former Hells Angel. He cannot erase his past, nor does he want to. But his past is no longer the defining signature of who he is today.

"I don't believe we have a South Asian or a Somali problem," Joe says emphatically, "even though that's often how it is por-trayed by the media, education authorities and police. I say to the youth I work with, 'Own it. Take responsibility. Give back to your communities. Be a part of the solution.' We were sixty shootings deep in 2015. Will this change? Is it going to get bet-ter? It's up to our youth.

"I grew up on the east side of Vancouver. I was what we called a 'parker,' guys who were identified by the different parks in which they congregated in groups. At eighteen, I was a competitive martial artist. I loved to fight—three or four per week—and loved rock and roll. But that was a different time. You got punched, you hit the ground, the fight was over. Nobody took it upon himself to stab you or kick you when you were down or, worse yet, shoot you. It was over."

Steele interjects. "When Joe and I look back over our upbringings, they really were not that different. We both grew up with parents who grappled with significant challenges. We both identified with our friends at the time more than we did with our families. But for me, there was one pivotal person who said, 'I'm not going to let bad things happen to you.' That person led me away from the temptations of gang life, even to the point of providing counselling to my entire family. The pivotal person in Joe's life led him in an entirely different direction, directly into the gang lifestyle—took hold of him, as it were, and said, 'This is the journey we are going to go on.' Joe went one way; I went the other. We became enemies."

Steele tells the students about the fight he and Joe had on Smithe Street and the infamous Calendino birthday where Joe was removed from the venue for failure to produce ID.

"Even to this day, Joe hates the fact I won the fight." Steele smiles. The students laugh, some nervously, as Joe steps forward, his face flushed with mock anger. "Pause," says Joe as he gives a timeout signal. He shakes his head, then picks up the story from his point of view.

"For those of you who don't know much about the Hells Angels, don't think for a second that you can go and knock on a Hells Angels clubhouse door and say, 'I am here and ready to join. Give me my patch.' I'm not going to get into details, but to give you a parallel, it's like a junior hockey league player in the Western Hockey League being able to make a National Hockey

League roster. It's amazing how many people think becoming a full-patch member is a logical and easy step. Truth be told, very few actually make it."

A smile crosses Joe's face.

"Another point of clarification. Brandon Steele did not take me down by himself on Smithe Street. There was Brandon and nine of his henchmen. I hated the very essence of Brandon and Kieron. I . . . could . . . not . . . stand . . . them." Joe lets each word drop like a blacksmith's hammer on an anvil. "One more thing. One New Year's Eve, Kieron introduced me to a stairwell, and then a ride and then a drop-off. You can fill in the blanks for yourself."

Steele interrupts the students' laughter by underlining that the Joe Calendino standing in front of the group is not the same person who was known to almost every member of the Vancouver Police Department. "Joe was very, very good at being very, very bad," he tells them.

"In the work I do with youth, I find that very few experts speak to them honestly," Joe continues. "Warning: You may end up in jail. Warning: You may end up a drug addict. Warning: You may end up dead. What so many of these impressionable youth get is the before picture. I strip away the BS. I tell it like it is."

Steele chimes in. "Ultimately, Joe provides a voice that police officers and educators cannot. We are very predictable. Students know what we're going to say. 'Don't do drugs.' 'You are going to go to jail.' 'You are going to die.' When you have somebody who has lived that life and has the perspective of having lived that life, you're able to reach out to that one kid in the crowd who will listen to a Joe but tune out anyone who smacks of establishment. Joe is able to say to that one student, 'I see myself in you. I am here for you.'"

Joe picks it up from there. "Yo Bro Yo Girl is all about the connections, getting the kids engaged, fostering a sense of ownership, a sense of belonging. We want to create opportunities for them and provide a forum where they can truly be heard—allow them to have a voice. My philosophy is simple: Give students the opportunity and they will shine."

Joe and Brandon give the last word to a young twenty-something gangster who appears via video. His words are haunting. "Once you're in, there's no way out," he tells the camera. "You either end up dead or in jail. You just keep getting used and used and used."

Almost predictably, Joe tells the students, the young man was later shot and killed, another casualty of the lifestyle that somehow spared Joe for greater things.

THE RESPECT JOE shows young people is evident in his interactions with parents too. He never talks down to anyone, and he keeps his words to a minimum. He would rather listen to what others have to say.

At a martial arts meet involving Yo Bro Yo Girl youth and hundreds of other young people from across Greater Vancouver, parents lauded the work Joe does.

"Without Joe's intervention," said one father, "our family would be in a mess. Drugs, defiance, anger: Joe has helped turn our son's life around in ways we as parents were not able to do. Now we get along great with our son."

Kind-hearted. Protective. Genuine. These are some of the qualities people identify with Joe today. Joe knew compassion in the gang world could mean death, and he made sure that his was rarely if ever on display. Now he understands, and communicates to others, that compassion means life.

Brenda describes an encounter she witnessed after one of Joe's presentations. "On one occasion, a well-dressed, middle-aged husband and wife approached Joe. They tried to hide their tears as they described the terrible dilemma they were facing. Their daughter was dating a young man who was waist-deep in gang life. What should they do? What could they do? they asked.

"Joe hearkened to his own days of gang involvement and shared with the couple what his parents did and did not do at the time. They continued to love him unequivocally, despite the contempt they held for some of the decisions he had made and the effect those decisions were having on their family life and their son's life.

"'Love your daughter,' Joe advised them. 'Don't ever throttle back on that. Just continue to love her, and let her know that you will not turn away from her. The easiest thing to do right now is close the door when times get tough. I get the fact they are tough for you right now. But fight that temptation. Keep the door open—always.'

"Simple advice, I know. But with Joe, he keeps it simple so there is no room for misunderstanding. He knows what worked for him, and he knows what will work for others."

Whether he's presenting to a prison population, a group of Junior A hockey players, a gathering of honour-roll students or a group of school dropouts, Joe makes connections. At a conference where he repeated his workshop several times, the same young man appeared at each session.

Joe approached the young man as the last session ended and asked him, "How would you like to go for a walk?"

They talked as they strolled, and Joe discovered that what this young man wanted was to share his own story—his concerns about the direction his life was taking and what he should do. Joe listened. He didn't form judgments. He waited until the young man had completed the entire choppy account of his life. Only then did Joe respond, not in a paternalistic "I know better" kind of way but supportively, by sharing his own experience—what had worked for him and what had not; how he'd determined who was a true friend and who was a false one;

how the decisions you make today have ramifications tomorrow, even years from now. Most importantly, Joe put a caring
arm around the young man's shoulders and reassured him.
"Remember, I'm here to help you. Don't hesitate to phone, text
or email me, whatever the circumstances and whatever the time
of day. I'm here for you."

Brenda stresses that the deep connections Joe makes are not
one-offs. They happen over and over again. To reinforce the
point, she tells a story about a time Joe came to meet her after
she'd completed a workshop at a hotel in downtown Vancouver.

"Joe had finished his work for the day, so he came to the hotel
to join me for dinner. As we sat there enjoying the moment, the
restaurant's chef appeared at our table. He greeted Joe warmly,
delighted to see him. Then, when Joe had gone to the washroom,
the chef began tearing up and said, 'Joe is like a brother to me.'
This happens all the time."

Joe and Brenda try not to look too far ahead, but the road
they're travelling is rewarding for both of them. They are
dedicated to their work and to each other, whatever the final
destination turns out to be.

19

HUMAN history is rife with bad predictions. There is the famous utterance attributed to Thomas Watson, former president of IBM, that "there's a world market for maybe five computers." There's the statement attributed to a former Decca Records executive Dick Rowe, who, after listening to the demo of a new band out of Liverpool, England, said dismissively, "We don't like their sound, and guitar music is on the way out." And there was the amazingly inaccurate prophesy of one of the great minds of all times, Albert Einstein: "There is not the slightest indication that nuclear energy will ever be obtainable. It would mean that the atom would have to be shattered at will."

Nobody can say for sure what the future will hold, and that's as true of Yo Bro Yo Girl and Joe Calendino as of anything else. Given Joe's personal success and the organization's success to date, it would be easy to say that both will continue to grow and flourish. Of course, saying something and achieving it are two different things.

For the organization to flourish, Joe has to flourish as well. He must continue his commitment to working with youth and constantly re-examine ways to expand and improve on the work he does. Always, in the background, lurks the bogeyman of addiction, as is the case for everyone who has ever kicked a habit. The same goes for the graduates of the Yo Bro Yo Girl program. Each of them must make the decision over and over again to stay on the path they have chosen.

Nonetheless, Joe holds resolutely to the goal he shared with Kevin Torvik as he lay curled in a concrete holding cell in Surrey: "Someday, I want to work with kids so that they don't have to go through this."

At the time, Joe's goal seemed as unlikely as computers in every home, a group of four lads from Liverpool becoming the most iconic band in rock history and nuclear power being harvested from the fusion of atoms. But from a not-quite-believable beginning, what was once Joe's dream has become a reality.

The final word on Joe's story will not be found in this book. Nor should it be. His journey continues, leading him through the inevitable ups and downs of life. Where it will take him, no one can say with certainty. What's indisputable, though, is this. Whatever the outcome for Joe, it is secondary to the outcomes for the hundreds, perhaps thousands, of people on whose lives Joe will have a positive impact. They will be better off for having known him. They will benefit because, at the lowest point in his life, Joe Calendino made a commitment to serve them—and succeeded in doing so. Joe has been to hell and back. He never wants to return.

ACKNOWLEDGEMENTS

I WAS honoured when Joe asked me to tell his story, despite my protestations that a professional writer would be more capable of doing his story justice. I'm not a wordsmith, merely someone who believes in the potential of every person to change and to influence others in ways both positive and profound. Joe is a shining example.

There are many people to acknowledge. For Joe, those people include Kevin Torvik, whom Joe credits with saving his life; Brenda Calendino, Joe's partner in life; the Odd Squad's Toby Hinton and Brian Shipper; Joe's family, who remained loyal and hopeful even when things looked bleakest; friends who stood with him through times good and bad; and Theresa Campbell and Rob Rai, dedicated individuals charged with helping students and their professional colleagues build safe schools and, ultimately, safe societies.

For my part, I would like to acknowledge the support and importance of friends too numerous to mention and my own family: my incredible partner, Maureen, who encourages me to dream big despite our family moniker; our daughter, Alanna, and son, Mike; my brothers, Bob and Jim, whose daughter,

Elizabeth, a noted writer, encouraged me to take on this project rather than pestering her to do so; and Susan Howell, a valued colleague and friend, whose encouragement to tell this story will forever be cherished. I would also like to thank our editor, Barbara Pulling, for her inestimable contributions, Jesse Finkelstein and the staff of Page Two Strategies, and, most importantly, Joe himself.

During an email exchange in early 2010, I replied to Joe, "I believe." I borrowed the phrase from the highly successful Winter Olympics that had just taken place in Vancouver. The words capture not only the dreams of the athletes who participated but also the aspirations of the innumerable Joes of the world who believe in their dreams. In the end, they are the ones who really count.

GARY LITTLE
Vancouver, British Columbia
February 24, 2017

SPECIAL THANKS

Special thanks to the volunteer board of YBYG, without whose expertise and generous assistance we would not be able to do the work we do in supporting our youth.

For the latest information regarding the Yo Bro Yo Girl Youth Initiative, access the organization's website at **www.ybyg.ca**

ABOUT THE AUTHORS

Joe Calendino (left) has over eight years of experience working with youth in some of Vancouver's most vulnerable neighbour-hoods as the founder and executive director of Yo Bro Yo Girl Youth Initiative. Along with his business degree, Joe holds a Substance Use Certificate from the Justice Institute of BC and is a certified black belt in Jiu Jitsu.

Gary Little (right) is an educator whose roles have included teacher, principal and Associate Superintendent of Schools, Vancouver School Board. Currently he is Director of International Baccalaureate Educator Programs at the Faculty of Education, University of British Columbia. In the mid-1980s, Gary was Joe Calendino's counsellor at Templeton Secondary School.

Page Two team members Gabrielle Narsted,
Jesse Finkelstein, and Peter Cocking

Page Two is a publishing agency that helps authors and organizations publish game-changing non-fiction books of the highest calibre. We are trusted industry experts with decades of experience and a passion for innovation. We turn experts into authors and help organizations produce beautiful books that express their mission and brand. We work with some of the most respected authors, thought leaders, and organizations in North America—and beyond. Our clients are writers, entrepreneurs, subject-matter experts, foundations and charitable organizations, business leaders, and innovators: people with deep expertise and something original to say.